br@in-based teaching

:)in the digital age

br@in-based teaching
:)in the digital age

Marilee Sprenger

Alexandria, Virginia USA

1703 N. Beauregard St. • Alexandria, VA 22311-1714 USA
Phone: 800-933-2723 or 703-578-9600 • Fax: 703-575-5400
Web site: www.ascd.org • E-mail: member@ascd.org
Author guidelines: www.ascd.org/write

Gene R. Carter, *Executive Director;* Nancy Modrak, *Publisher;* Scott Willis, *Director, Book Acquisitions & Development;* Carolyn Pool, *Acquisitions Editor;* Julie Houtz, *Director, Book Editing & Production;* Leah Lakins, *Editor;* Catherine Guyer, *Senior Graphic Designer;* Mike Kalyan, *Production Manager;* Keith Demmons, *Typesetter*

All Web links in this book are correct as of the publication date below but may have become inactive or otherwise modified since that time. If you notice a deactivated or changed link, please e-mail books@ascd.org with the words "Link Update" in the subject line. In your message, please specify the Web link, the book title, and the page number on which the link appears.

PAPERBACK ISBN: 978-1-4166-0918-6   ASCD product # 110018   n3/10

Also available as an e-book (see Books in Print for the ISBNs).

Quantity discounts for the paperback edition only: 10–49 copies, 10%; 50+ copies, 15%; for 1,000 or more copies, call 800-933-2723, ext. 5634, or 703-575-5634. For desk copies: member@ascd.org.

Library of Congress Cataloging-in-Publication Data

Sprenger, Marilee, 1949-
  Brain-based teaching in the digital age / Marilee Sprenger.
     p. cm.
  Includes bibliographical references and index.
  ISBN 978-1-4166-0918-6 (pbk. : alk. paper) 1. Learning, Psychology of. 2. Brain.
  3. Computer-assisted instruction 4. Classroom environment I. Title.
  LB1057.S66 2010
  370.15'23–dc22

                              2009042848

20 19 18 17 16 15 14 13 12 11 10   1 2 3 4 5 6 7 8 9 10 11 12

Dedication

This book is dedicated to the memory of Kindra Buchanan McLennan who bravely shared her story of life and death with the world through her blog. She hoped that by reaching out on a global level she would help other young women who face the battle she so valiantly tried to win. Her spirit remains with all those who knew and loved her.

br@in-based teaching
:)in the digital age

Acknowledgments

I would like to acknowledge the following people who have made this book possible:

To my husband, Scott, thank you for everything that you do. You keep me grounded. Your support and love are what keep me writing and speaking. I love you.

To my son, Josh, and my daughter-in-law, Amy, you inspire me with your knowledge of technology, your ability to fix those digital problems, and your creativity in your great online company. Even though you are part of Generation X, you have managed to keep up with the Net Geners.

To Marnie, my daughter, and Thabu, my son-in-law, you are global learners in many ways. As members of the Net Generation, you characterize the necessity of globalization as you work with people and family all over the world from your digital devices.

To my grandchildren, Jack and Emmie, you are part of Generation Next. Although you are too young yet to be dabbling digitally, you have watched your parents, aunt and uncle, and grandparents as we have defined ourselves in technological ways. It is an honor to be a part of your lives and watch you grow. We can talk about you becoming firefighters, doctors, senators, or professional athletes, but your lives will be much different from life as we know it today. My work is to ensure that each of you is received at your schools as a whole child and that somehow we create personal education plans to prepare you for the rest of the 21st century and beyond.

To Carolyn Pool and Scott Willis from the book acquisitions department at ASCD, thank you for your encouragement and your enthusiasm about this book project. I have always enjoyed working with you both. The amazing work of Deborah Siegel and Leah Lakins cannot go unnoticed. Thanks for doing such a great job editing my book.

And finally, to the digital natives who have made the world a better place and who take the time to teach us digital immigrants how to survive and thrive in a global world. Thank you for being my teachers.

Introduction

I am doing some research and ordering a book from Amazon.com that contains a review of several studies I need for my project. I am tempted to check the box for one-day shipping so I can have the material in my hands by tomorrow evening. I think to myself, "What the heck! Another $3.99 and I can continue my work in 24 hours." I willingly decide to spend the extra money on shipping, enter my credit card information, and hit the "Place my order" button. Without delay, I am sent to a "Thank you for your order" page that presents me with a confirmation number and assures me that I will receive an order confirmation via e-mail within 24 hours. (In fact, in seconds I hear a click, and a "You've got mail!" message comes through my speakers loud and clear.) I decide I do not need to print this page as my e-mail confirmation has arrived and will contain the information I need to trace my order. In reality, I have an account with Amazon, as many of you do, and with my handy screen name and password I can track all of my orders, print out receipts, and keep track of my expenditures with the company. Isn't technology great?

I am about to leave this page when I notice an interesting option. If I am interested in reading this book *right now*, I can read the book online for a mere $7.95. It will be in a format that makes it impossible for me to print, but I can get a jump start on my research. How clever of them to offer this to me *after* I have paid $40 for the paperback book! However, I am always in a hurry, curious about the research, and obviously not very prudent about expenditures, so I eagerly press the purchase button again. Within seconds, my credit card is charged and I am reading current information on a topic I will soon be presenting at a conference.

Cool! I have paid extra money to get my hands on . . . well, not really my hands; and this part makes me uncomfortable with my resource. I love books. I love to read. I greet and handle my books in a loving way. I'm one of those crazy people who love to look at the cover, the spine, and the back of a book. I check out the index before the table of contents. I sometimes peruse a book from back to front. I smell my books. This is not a fetish, nor am I kinky in any way. Some of you, like me, are baby boomers; we remember the smell of freshly printed books. They aren't quite the same anymore with the new processes printers use, but old habits are hard to break.

So here I am, looking at my book on a screen. I can't smell it or feel the cover beneath my fingers, nor can I get out my highlighter and mark the essentials I am seeking. As my eyes scan the print on the screen and I scroll from page to page, thoughts are quickly entering my memory and leaving just as fast. "Oh, that's important; I'll remember to find that tomorrow when the real book arrives. Shall I take notes? Too much trouble when it will all be at my beck and call tomorrow. What interesting information! I need to underline something. I need to stick a sticky note here and there. I'd even fold a corner down if I could." (Book lovers, I know this is a sacrilege, but I am feeling desperate.)

My brain tries hard to fit in to the techno era. I can use my laptop like a pro in many ways. I own two iPods. I use a Smartphone, which, by the way, is much smarter than I am! I gave up my paper calendar years ago. But a book . . . a book is another story altogether. A book comes alive when I hold it in my hands, when I smell it and mark in it. I get to write my name in it. I doodle, draw arrows, make stars, and I take notes in the backs of my books. Is there something wrong with my brain that I so dislike this process of reading a book on a screen?

My students and my children have no problem reading books on their computers or on their Kindles, the digital reader offered by Amazon. They can highlight on their Kindles, so I have been tempted to step into that area of digital geography. But I'm not ready. Not yet. And my brain isn't either.

The authors of *iBrain* (Small & Vorgan, 2008) call people like me "digital immigrants," but I feel more like a digital dinosaur. We didn't grow up with the new technology, so as adults our brains are trying to adjust. Because our brains are so malleable as a result of their neuroplasticity, they will change as we accept the challenge and the excitement of catching up in the 21st century. My son, Josh, is 33, and his sister, Marnie, is 31. Josh is a member of Generation X, the most educated group in history. Marnie's age puts her on the cusp between the Gen Xers and the Net Generation. Sometimes the Net Generation is called Generation Y. For those born from 1998 to the present, we refer to Generation Next, also known as Generation Z. The Net Gens are digital natives who have grown up in this digital era. Nothing scares them about technology. Nothing surprises them. In fact, their expectations are such that this is all very normal. Why read a book any other way than on a computer, an iPod, or a Smartphone? Or watch a television show? Or a movie?

I have a feeling that some of you had trouble following me in that last paragraph. You are wondering what generation you are in. You are wondering if you are teachings *X*s, *Y*s, or *Z*s. And in your hearts, you hope you are teaching *A*s, *B*s, and *C*s! Refer to Figure I.1 for some clarification. I know I will!

Figure I.1	Generations of Technology Users	
Year of Birth	**Popular Name**	**Learning Environment**
1946–1964	TV Generation (Baby Boomers)	Passive
1965–1976	Generation X	Holds the highest education levels
1977–1998	Generation Y (Net Generation or Net Gens)	Grew up using computers
1999–	Generation Z	First generation to have seen their parents embrace technology as they do

It's time we all met the "digital brains." They are in our classrooms, teachers' rooms, and boardrooms. They are here to stay, just as brain research is. Instead of focusing on what's wrong with this new era, let's get into the 21st century. We need to use the technology tools, learn the digital dialogue, and understand and relate better to our students. The key to learning is relationships. Many of our students have strong relationships with and through these digital devices. By creating our own relationships with these instruments, we will build stronger relationships with our students.

Let us not forget, though, that movement, art, music, and play still belong in the classroom. This book asks you to seek understanding, but also balance.

In Part 1 of the book, I tell you how digital technology is changing the brain and discuss what's new and applicable from brain research. In this section, I also explain how some of the brain-based teaching principles apply in the digital world. In Part 2 of the book, I talk about the whole child, learning environments, and the importance of group learning. Part 3 covers music, mind mapping, and memory. In Part 4, I explore the topic of how to try to balance 21st century technological skills with people skills and look at some options for what future learning will be like. Each chapter includes "instant messages" with bits of useful information.

Throughout this book, we will focus on the need for our students to have emotional intelligence, creativity, and the ability to synthesize information to be successful in a world that is changing from an information age to a conceptual age. I ask you to consider the material presented here, whether you are a digital native or a digital immigrant. The brain is changing, and so can you.

PART 1

Digital Technology and the Brain

What is technology doing to the brain? The importance of 21st century skills coupled with what research has discovered about the brain creates an opportunity to combine brain-compatible strategies that will work with our diverse populations. Both digital natives and digital immigrants must survive and thrive in this very connected world.

CHAPTER 1

iPod + iPhone + iVideo + Internet = iBrain

One of my middle school students was texting her friend sitting next to her in study hall. The girls began laughing, so I asked what was so funny. She shared this text message with me. "First, he left me a voicemail, so I sent him a text on his cell; then, he contacted me on Facebook, so I e-mailed him on my BlackBerry. Two days later he sent me an instant message on AOL, but I wasn't online. How will I ever meet him?" This is the life of the digital brain. Face-to-face contact is not necessarily required! And herein lies one of the warnings about technology: our students may be lacking face-to-face social skills.

Various authors, including Gary Small (Small & Vorgan, 2008), call them "digital natives"; others, including Don Tapscott (2009), call them the Net Generation, or Net Gen; and we've called them geeks and nerds. Who are they? Your students. And maybe you, too.

The Changing World of Digital Interaction

When on playground duty at the middle school in the morning, I am amazed at the changes I have seen in the past 10 years. Students stand together in circles just like they used to, but they aren't speaking to each other. Instead, they are sending text messages—to the people they are standing with. It's more fun, they say. And they can text things they don't want to say out loud.

Once these students enter the building, their cell phones must be turned off. We can't have students texting each other in class. They have to be paying attention to the lesson. The question is, can they? Or will they? How can a teacher be as interesting as a communications tool that can take students anywhere they want to go—MySpace, outer space, or cyberspace?

The facility with which most students approach the digital age is awe-inspiring. While I am still at the stage of believing the way to fix my computer is to reboot, our students are opening multiple windows and using advanced programs to make things happen. (If when you read "opening multiple windows" you thought I was referring to letting in fresh air, you must keep reading!) They have staked out their personal territory on MySpace or Facebook. They talk to people around the world using Skype, and they have their own Web sites, blogs, and wikis. If you think I am speaking a foreign language, be patient; these terms will be explained throughout this book.

You need to know the language, the programs, and your students better. Knowing their world means being familiar with cyberspace, text messaging, and an informal language that makes you LOL (that's "laugh out loud").

The Changing Brain

We know that the brain is changing in response to the changes brought about by the high-tech information age in which we live. If we want brain-compatible classrooms, we need to know what these changes are—the good, the bad, and the ugly—just as we want our doctor to keep up with the latest treatments and medications, our accountant to keep up with the tax laws, and our mechanic to know how to keep our computer-regulated cars in good shape.

According to Jensen (2005), teachers must be experts on the organ that they teach—the brain. New information about the brain can have a profound effect on the classroom if teachers are aware of it (Allen, Nickelsen, & Zgonc, 2007). Many administrators feel that the first professional development their teachers participate in should focus on how the brain learns. Although it is not necessary to know a lot about brain biology, there are some essentials that the brain-compatible teacher should know in the digital age, which presents us with a new kind of diversity in our classrooms: students who have been exposed to various kinds of digital equipment and communications systems, and students (and teachers) who have not.

If you need a refresher on how the brain learns, you'll find it in Appendix A (see p. 151). But it's also important to know how students' brains are changing and working now. How do their brains learn best? What can we do to compete with the attractions of the digital age? Better yet, how can we join the digital age? Becoming a part of this transformation is something we must do because we are dealing with digital brains. So even if you are a digital dinosaur, it's not too late. Your brain can change, too. In fact, it's changing every day.

The Reticular Activating System: A Busy Filter

Brain research during the past 20 years indicates notable changes in parts of the brain, including the reticular activating system (RAS), which is the brain's first filter. Located in the area of the brain associated with survival activities, it scans the outside world for danger and determines which information is allowed to enter the brain. Because the brain is programmed to forget, the RAS filters out about 99 percent of the incoming information (Gazzaniga, 1999). This selectivity usually allows us to focus and keep our sanity.

Our students live in a world of constant messaging, and therefore their brains—their reticular activating systems—have changed more than ours. Fast-paced, emotionally laden messages bombard them regularly from computers, videos, and other technology, and the RAS has changed as a result of this overexposure. Because of the increase in the number and pace of messages, the RAS scans more quickly and expects more information. We may see the effect when we are teaching our students; their engagement may be brief, as new stimuli are discovered by the

RAS. If you do not find yourself "performing" more in your classroom or putting on a "dog and pony show" to get your students' attention, then you are in the minority.

Digital Dopamine

The neurotransmitter dopamine is released in the brain when we feel pleasure. Ask your Net Gen students what they like and you'll probably hear responses that refer to a variety of digital activities and devices, such as texting, instant messaging, and playing Nintendo, Xbox, PlayStation, or Wii. They may mention iPods, iPhones, cruising the Internet, and watching HDTV. Because the brain craves novelty, excitement, and innovation, it naturally turns to things that are new and different, and technology offers much of this kind of stimulation.

As Judy Willis (2006) tells us, we have to get the dopamine flowing in our students' brains when they are learning. Pleasure must be part of the learning. But technology isn't the only source of pleasure. It behooves us to include both high-tech and low-tech activities in our lessons to encourage pleasurable experiences. For example, movement encourages the release of dopamine and can be incorporated into certain learning activities.

Pruning Traditional Language Pathways

The more our students are actively involved with the new technology, the more their brains are changing. Texting, e-mailing, and instant messaging call for a new kind of language. It is an abbreviated form of verbal communication that originally horrified me as a teacher of grammar, spelling, punctuation, and writing. I have calmed down over the years as I see that the world has not come to an end as a result of this insult to my language, my content area, and my life. In fact, I have grown quite used to it, and I even understand much of it.

R U reading this? If you are, TIA. If you aren't, OMG! Get a life!

Translation? "Are you reading this? If you are, thanks in advance. If you aren't, oh my gosh (god)! Get a life!"

As educators, we know it behooves us to enter our students' worlds. This form of interaction *is* the world to many of them. I am suggesting you change your brain. You probably think, as I once did, that you are part of this technological era because you use e-mail. I have quickly learned that e-mail is becoming as passé as snail mail. Texting, blogging, and messaging are the mediums of choice. Try it; you might like it! LOL.

Meanwhile, as our students are using their changing brains, some of the old connections—the neural networks—are slowly fading. The traditional communication skills need to be used to solidify those neural networks. The Net Geners may ask, "Why?" And my answer to them is that the whole world hasn't changed yet. They will still be in classrooms that require traditional learning. Colleges and universities have lots of technology, but students still will be required to write an essay that flows, a story with a beginning, a middle, and an ending; and they may even have to write (I know this is hard to swallow) a formal letter!

Digital Dilemmas

There are some aspects to the digital world that are causes for concern. It seems that every year we see more students with attention problems. Now, there are questions about technology stunting brain growth, losing emotional intelligence skills, multitasking, developing reading skills, and acquiring general knowledge. The digital brain may encounter some issues that we will need to address.

Frontal Lobe Lethargy

Our frontal lobes are the last lobes to develop completely as the brain grows. They perform executive functions such as abstract thinking, future planning, and decision making. They also are involved in our social interactions. To the surprise of some researchers, playing video games does not activate the frontal lobe. Even games that are more complex tend to stimulate the visual and motor functions in the brain, not the frontal lobes (Small & Vorgan, 2008). Interestingly, researchers have found that doing ordinary addition problems activated many more brain areas, including the frontal lobe.

Adolescents who are completely immersed in technology may suffer from stunted frontal lobe development. Social abilities are not maturing as students between the ages of 8 and 18 spend 8 ½ hours per day with digital media (Klingberg,

2008). Their ability to empathize and relate to others is delayed as their neural networks focus on a faceless world without gestures.

Attention

As noted earlier, the brain is fueled by the need to encounter something new and different. Novelty is important to us. This is one reason why the technological revolution continues to engage our students—and many of us as well. As we scan our world for new things, the amount of attention we give to any one of them is dwindling. The average person spends about two seconds per Web site when doing a search. We have become experts at seeking out the information we want and are able to peruse a Web page quickly as we scan for specific words and concepts.

As our students work at their computers outside of school, they await instant messages and e-mails from their friends. Their anticipation is likely to cause stress as they hope to be contacted and think about this possibility while they try to do their work. Stress causes the release of stress hormones, and as they finish their work, many students have higher stress levels than when they began.

The need for connectivity is heightened under these circumstances—the waiting and the wondering: *Will she text me back? Did he see that I am online, and is he avoiding me? Where is everyone while I am doing my work?* Even those of us who do not yet rely on these instant connections get caught up in this tendency. I check my "friend" list when I log in to my message page. I feel more connected to my own children and to my friends when I see their screen names listed as "online." We all have the need to feel in control of our lives, and when we don't have that feeling, it can affect our self-worth.

INSTANT MESSAGE

As students divide their attention among various tasks, their sense of control over their lives may be threatened, adding more stress to their lives. They need some downtime to balance their brains. Interacting with real people face to face, taking short naps, and exercising may be beneficial.

Depression

Jane Healy warned us about the problem of depression in her book *Failure to Connect* (1998). She reminded readers that the brain responds to its environment, that computer usage in isolation limits language development, that lack of physical exercise affects brain growth and stimulation, and that there may be more incidences of depression by students living in a more isolated world.

When communication is limited to texting, e-mailing, instant messaging, and blogging, emotional warmth is lacking. In particular, those who are new to technology—the digital immigrants—notice the isolation and depression more than digital natives (Small & Vorgan, 2008).

Social-Emotional Intelligence: Lost in Cyberspace?

The ability to understand, recognize, and handle our own emotions, recognize others' emotions, and manage relationships are all components of emotional intelligence. Add impulse control and empathy and you have the characteristics of a student we would all like to have in our schools and classrooms.

Daniel Goleman (2006) defines social intelligence as a combination of social awareness and social facility. These traits involve listening to others, understanding their feelings, responding to their gestures and facial expressions, interacting nonverbally, and responding to their needs.

These social and emotional skills are learnable, as we have seen through wonderful school programs and brain-compatible schools where they are a priority. These skills are built through face-to-face encounters and are nearly impossible to learn through digital technology. Yes, webcams and Skype can provide some face time, but body language and gestures are sometimes lost in these high-tech interactions. A lack of social skills can be a side effect of too much time spent with technology.

Multitasking—or Not?

According to many neuroscientists, including John Medina (2008), multitasking is not only unproductive, it is impossible. The brain can attend to only one thing at a time. Multitasking is unfeasible for the brain. Yes, we can walk and talk at the same time, but those two processes do not involve the same brain functions. Walking is a procedural motor memory. It has become automatic; we don't have to think about it. The executive part of our brain can focus on the conversation.

Let's look at what happens in Emily's brain as she thinks she is focusing on her homework:

Emily sits in front of her laptop. Her iPod is playing music by Coldplay as it sits in its base on her dresser. She has three windows open on her computer screen: AOL, MSN Messenger, and her word processing program. Her homework is to write about five causes for the Civil War and support them with details.

As Emily is putting her heading on her paper, her cell phone rings. She quickly picks up her BlackBerry, recognizes the caller by the programmed music that plays for that person, and sees the picture of her caller appear as she says, "Hi, Ivy. What's up?" Ivy begins the conversation by saying, "You're not going to believe who texted me!" Emily is absorbed in the conversation and squeals as she hears the familiar name of someone Ivy is interested in dating.

Just as Em is about to respond to Ivy, her computer spouts out, "You've got mail!" and she turns her attention to the newest e-mail message. The executive part of her brain drops the conversation (though Ivy keeps talking), and Emily reads the e-mail from another classmate asking her what the homework assignment is. Em replies with the page numbers and the assignment as Ivy rambles, but she realizes that she should get back to her homework. "I'll text you later, Ivy. I have to get some work done."

Emily shifts her attention back to the computer screen. "Let's see, where was I?" she wonders. Now her brain must let the snippets of social conversation drop out of her working memory. Attending to her homework on the Civil War causes her brain to retrieve some long-term memories of her readings and teacher lectures on the topic. As she begins to think about the differences between the North and the South before the Civil War, her mind drifts to *Gone with the Wind* and how cute Rhett Butler was.

Refocusing takes several seconds as she remembers what Mr. Montgomery told them in class about the slaves. Emily types "causes of the Civil War" into Google. Immediately, the search engine provides 12,900,000 hits. She clicks on the first site listed, realizes it doesn't have any information she is looking for, hits the "back" button, and tries the next Web site. Deep into her search, she is startled by the familiar sound from her BlackBerry indicating that she has a text message. She grabs her phone, presses the mail button, and sees Jackson's message: "What r u doing?" Jackson is special, so her brain turns its attention to possibilities of love. Her brain is flooded with pleasurable chemicals that keep her from returning to her homework as she begins typing her reply.

And so it goes with the Net Generation. Multitasking? Not many tasks are actually getting done. Later, however, Emily will remember that her mission was to complete her homework, and she will stay up late attempting to explain the reasons for the Civil War.

Some researchers believe that rather than multitasking, what Emily is doing is putting herself into a state of partial attention. Linda Stone, a former software executive for Microsoft, has examined attention and coined the phrase "continuous partial attention" (Stone, 2007). Digital natives are motivated by a desire to be busy and in demand. They don't want to miss anything. Being physically present has become less important. Instead of multitasking and trying to be productive, it is more important to be connected. This "overconnectedness" can cause stress.

Stress results in the release of two chemicals from the adrenal glands, cortisol and adrenaline. Initially, this chemical release may enhance memory. But over time, stress chemicals can weaken the immune system, weaken cognitive functioning, and in some cases cause depression.

Net Geners think more quickly than their older counterparts. In a Oxford Future of the Mind Institute study, Net Geners scored up to 10 percent higher on problem solving than older people, which of course may be attributed to age differences and high exposure to fast-paced technology. Some studies suggest, however, that when Net Geners are interrupted, they think and work at about the same speed as people in their 30s. Some research concludes that those who were raised with digital media can switch attention faster and have optimized their ability to multitask. Is this a good thing? In most cases the answer is no. Researchers believe that this does not make them more productive, creative, or inventive, and perhaps makes them less so than those without the interruptions (Scott, 2006). Studies show that interruptions can cause 50 percent more errors and take people 50 percent longer to complete the task (Medina, 2008).

Differences in Reading Skills

Maryanne Wolf, author of *Proust and the Squid* (2007), is concerned about the need children feel for speed on the Internet and other digital devices when it comes to reading. As an expert in the neuroscience of reading, Wolf fears that as young children learn to read on equipment that is known for fast pace and skimming, they will lose their ability to truly comprehend and reflect on the text they are encountering.

Wolf believes that the love of reading comes from some interaction with books, just as I do. In her book, she says that learning to read begins when a baby is held in the caregiver's arms and is read to with love. If that first encounter with reading is in front of a screen, will the baby feel bathed in love and develop a love of reading? Or is the issue that the digital immigrants are having trouble letting go of what we believe good reading is—the love of a good book that can be held and touched?

A study was conducted to see if computer-savvy people read differently than those who are computer naïve. Brain scans showed that, when reading text in books, both groups used the same neural connections for reading. A difference was seen, however, when the groups were searching the Internet using Google. Those with computer knowledge and skills used different neural networks than those with little computer experience. The tech-savvy people used part of the frontal cortex known as the dorsolateral prefrontal area. As the study continued, the brains of the inexperienced users changed, and in five days the newbies were using the same networks (Small & Vorgan, 2008).

Differences in Information Acquisition

In *Grown Up Digital*, Don Tapscott (2009) discusses the fact that Net Geners absorb information differently than any other generation. When they scan a Web site, their approach is keyed into visuals. They are accustomed to icons and other visuals and know they will provide information they need. Baby boomers, on the other hand, approach a Web site the way they were taught to read—begin in the upper left and look at the text.

A study was conducted in which news was presented to Net Geners in four ways: a traditional radio newscast, an online newscast launched with one click, an interactive webcast that allowed users to click on individual stories, and a webcast that included links to retrieve more information. The study participants remembered the least from the traditional newscast and more from those that were interactive.

The conclusion we can draw from these examples is that our students do not necessarily need to begin at the beginning and go through to the end. What a change that is from traditional learning!

Digital Dividends

There are pros to this wired life. If you talk to the Net Geners, they will make several points that do make sense. First, working and researching digitally in isolated situations causes one to appreciate social interactions when they do occur. Going out with friends is a need that must be filled. Second, these digital brains are really good at what they do. They know how to search and find the information they seek. The facility that young people have with computers and other forms of technology is beneficial in many of their school projects and their jobs.

Collaboration can be a by-product of our high-tech world. Students have the opportunity to collaborate with other students all over the world, but what about in the classroom? Teachers who insist that students work together on technology-based multimedia projects can help students develop emotional intelligences through the social interaction involved in working on projects.

Another potential dividend is the possibility of providing highly individualized instruction. We know that to get the best results in terms of student learning, we must differentiate content, process, product, and environment. Using various forms of technology offers students a "one size fits one" approach to learning. It also offers students choice, which is so important to the brain and learning. They can choose digital or nondigital ways of showing what they know.

Brain-compatible strategies are learning-compatible strategies. The use of technology for these changing brains is extremely compatible for learning. As the world of education changes from teacher centered to student centered, brain-compatible classrooms provide the foundation for learning.

Digital Dangers

I would be remiss if I didn't address the issue of inappropriate use of digital media. We hear horror stories about young people who display inappropriate pictures on their MySpace or Facebook pages. Some take pictures with their cell phones and, without thinking, send them to everyone on their address list. If we are going to help our students use technology, we must also teach them how to use it wisely. In this book, I am discussing the use of digital media for learning. I would hope that whoever is providing our students with the equipment they use for other purposes is also teaching them what is appropriate and what is not. We know this is not always the case. Visit the site wiredkids.org for valuable information for educators, parents, and students.

Addictive behavior is another potential danger. Addictive indicators include (1) preoccupation that causes users to think about their last Internet session or their next session, (2) lack of control that makes them unable to stop, (3) physical withdrawal symptoms as they try to cut back, and (4) staying online long after they intended to stop. To be considered addictive, these activities must be associated with one of the following actions: (1) interference with aspects of life such as work, school, or relationships; (2) telling lies to hide the activity; or (3) using the Internet as an escape to avoid personal problems or uncomfortable feelings (Small & Vorgan, 2008). In a study published by the Associated Press (2006) that tracked 2,500 subjects at Stanford University, 14 percent of the subjects who regularly used computers reported that it disrupted their lives and caused them to neglect school, work, sleep, eating, and family interactions.

The addictive possibilities of technology are endless, and it can affect people from all walks of life. Our students can become addicted to computer games and may spend hours playing them. In some of these games they can take on social roles, and the game becomes their fantasy life. Although most of our students don't have all of the criteria for addiction listed here, many of them enjoy the dopamine rush they get as they feel in control online. They may not make good decisions if their brains just want to get "back to the game" or whatever site they crave.

Of course, there are other addictions related to the Internet. We have all read about sexual addictions, gambling addictions, online shopping addictions, and even e-mail addictions!

Watch for signs in your students and others. Be sure to keep computers in public places to curtail an addictive activity. Help your students find a healthy balance between interactive technology and interaction with real people.

The Brains of Today and Tomorrow

According to Howard Gardner (2007), who examines skills needed for the 21st century and beyond in his book *Five Minds for the Future*, the minds that students will need are a disciplined mind, a synthesizing mind, a creative mind, a respectful mind, and an ethical mind. Daniel Pink (2005), author of *A Whole New Mind*, believes that two sets of skills that will make our students successful in our rapidly changing world are "high-concept" skills (the ability to detect patterns, connect unrelated ideas, and create something new), and "high-touch" skills (the ability to empathize, to read faces and gestures, to find joy in oneself, and extract it in others). For our students to be able to create, synthesize, and be respectful (create relationships), which both authors agree are important attributes for success in the 21st century, educators need to examine what it is that we already do to encourage the development of these types of minds and then create more such experiences and environments.

In the following chapters, I share current research that connects brain-compatible teaching to both digital and nondigital strategies. Trying to maintain a balance as we keep ourselves open to the strengths and the needs of our students will create classrooms that motivate, stimulate, and celebrate learning.

TEXT MESSAGE

The terms "digital natives" and "digital immigrants" were first coined in 2001 by Marc Prensky in a two-part article (see www.marcprensky.com/writing). Prensky believes that "digital wisdom" comes from not only expanding our capabilities through digital media but also using it wisely.
TIFN. (That's it for now.)

CHAPTER 2

Recent Research on the Brain: We Need Low Tech, Too

The research on the brain that is being done today uses high-tech instruments that can show the brain in action. Some areas of study conclude that students' brains need various kinds of activities. For instance, some suggest the positive outcomes of exercise and the arts on cognitive development. Your brain affects everything you do. If you take care of your brain, it will take care of you. If you abuse your brain, it will age and deteriorate more quickly.

Current research also suggests that the more you challenge your brain by learning new things, the better off your brain will be. Your brain will change by reading this page, this chapter, and this book. Hurray for you! Keep adding new ideas.

There are always new studies that suggest possible classroom applications of brain research. To be valid for classroom use, the research must be extensive, repeated, and relevant. The information in this chapter comes from reliable sources, has been studied and analyzed well, and has stood the test of time. These are topics currently being discussed at conferences by both neuroscientists and educators. Specifically, current research suggests the following:

- The brain contains mirror neurons that influence behaviors (Iacoboni, 2008).
- The brain is so changeable that it is referred to as "plastic," and educators are referred to as "neuroplasticians" (Doidge, 2007).
- Exercise increases test scores (Ratey, 2008).
- An interest in the arts has implications for different types of learning and memory (Medical News Today, 2008).
- Negative feedback affects brains differently (van Duijvenvorde et al., 2008)

Let's look at each of these topics in greater detail.

Mirror Neurons

It is after lunch and your students have just returned to class. You are standing in front of them feeling refreshed and ready to start the lesson. You look up, smiling, and begin to introduce the lesson. "We are going to discuss the reasons for the Civil War." The students are not as excited as you are, but you have a really interesting way to help them remember the information that you are anxious to share.

It has been a long day. Jeremy decided to go ballistic when you discussed the length of the term paper you assigned. You had to chase Cory down the hall to get him to take his Ritalin, as it was obvious that he had neglected to do so. You are tired; yet you are psyched! You look at Sally sitting in the first row. She has turned to talk to Brennan. She yawns and closes her eyes. Within seconds, you yawn. You look around the room and watch as several others in your vicinity also begin to yawn. What is happening?

Sometimes we feel tired after lunch, but the real "black hole" that our brains encounter doesn't occur until much later in the afternoon. But the phenomenon I just described can be explained by the discovery of a neuronal system in our brains called the mirror neuron system. It is aptly named because these networks of neurons in our brains begin to wire together when we watch someone do something. Consequently, our brains are then set up so that we do the exact same thing.

The research continues into this new understanding of one aspect of the brain. The research is relevant to the study of autism because it shows some differences in the way the autistic brain responds to stimuli. It appears that fewer mirror neurons are either present or activated in most autistic brains. Beyond the knowledge gained about disorders such as autism, the research on mirror neurons offers much to be considered in the educational arena.

Imitation by infants, such as sticking out their tongues when looking at an adult doing the same, is followed by toddler imitation. Studies have shown that when given the same objects to play with and manipulate, one toddler will imitate the other. Who does the most imitating? The toddler with the least amount of verbal language. A year or two later, the children who play more imitation games will develop fluent speech. Imitation appears to be the introduction to oral communication (Iacoboni, 2008).

The expression "Do what I say, not what I do" isn't going to work, according to this new research. We have to walk the talk because surely our students will imitate what we do. This conclusion has implications for learning in terms of both social interactions and content. As our students watch what we are doing, their brains mirror the action, and in so doing they know what will occur next.

For this very reason, research is being conducted on the use of gestures and their connection to learning. According to Estes (2008), communication is only 7 percent words; the remainder is divided between tonality, which accounts for 35 percent, and body language, which accounts for 58 percent. Therefore, it's not what we say that matters most, but how we say it and what we are doing when we say it. According to a new study (Goldin-Meadow, Cook, & Mitchell, 2009), gesturing helps students learn. Math is a content area that is frequently used in examples of gesturing and learning. If the teacher gestures in a way to assist students' understanding, learning takes place sooner. For an equation such as $4 + 6 = \_\_ + 8$, many students will look at the equal sign and assume they should add the 4, the 6, and the 8. If the teacher uses her hands to cup each side of the equation, she is indicating that each side is separate but that the sides are connected. A University of Rochester study (2007) found that students who learned with gesture remembered 90 percent of what they were taught compared to only 33 percent for those taught with speech only.

Have you ever finished someone's sentence for them? We think we only do that with someone we know very well. The research suggests otherwise. As our mirror neurons fire when others speak, they provide us with an idea of what will be said next (Sylwester, 2006). Usually we are right on target when we fill in a word or finish another person's sentence.

Exploration of mirror neurons is leading researchers to believe that these brain cells may be responsible for social, physical, and cognitive behavior. Your mirror neurons fire when you drive a car, see someone driving, hear a car, and even just when someone says something about driving a car. Imagine the implications for student learning through rehearsing in these multifaceted ways!

Educators as Neuroplasticians

The discovery that our brains have the ability to change is one of the most fascinating discoveries about the brain in centuries. As an educator, you change students' brains every day. In fact, the brain is the only organ that sculpts itself, and it does so through its experiences.

Throughout our lives the brain goes through periods of blooming and pruning. The blooming stages occur as dendrites, axons, and synapses grow. At birth, the 100 billion neurons do not have many connections, but by age 2, the brain has more connections than are needed, so pruning begins. In fact, by age 1, a child has twice as many connections as his or her mother (Begley, 2007).

The brain—especially the young brain—is so plastic that a child can have an entire hemisphere of the brain removed and still have most of the functions of both hemispheres. This is possible because the remaining hemisphere takes over those functions. If a baby is born with a cataract, as long as the cataract is removed by five months of age, the baby's vision will be fine (Eliot, 1999).

At age 10 or 12, the frontal lobe experiences a growth spurt, with a proliferation of new connections. This burst is in preparation for the many changes that will occur during adolescence, a time for young people to make choices and design their own brains. Both good and bad experiences will affect that design. Our students will determine whether they will sculpt a brain that excels at music and sports or one that will be changed by alcohol and drugs.

In most cases, what hasn't been learned before adolescence can still be learned during the second or third decade of life. As students learn and make new networks of neurons, their brains will change to support the new learning. With enough exposure to new concepts, skills, and facts, the memories will be permanently stored in their brains in a very retrievable fashion.

INSTANT MESSAGE

 As educators, we must remember that no two brains are alike—not the brains of siblings or even twins. Every brain is unique and has been created as a result of its own distinctive experiences. Every lesson that we teach will affect each student according to the information that has been stored in the individual brain.

Studies show that even thinking about learning can change the brain. Two groups of people were taught to play a particular song on the piano. After two weeks of practice, one group was told to continue practicing and the other group was to only think about playing the song. Both the thinkers and the doers showed expanded connections in their brains (Begley, 2007).

Exercise and the Brain

There is no doubt that exercise increases brain power. Studies clearly show that aerobic exercise improves cognitive function in brains of all ages. Blood flow and oxygen increase in the brain as circulation improves during exercise (Medina, 2008). Exercise also destroys "free radicals" that can cause your brain to deteriorate just as an apple exposed to air turns brown. Free radicals are leftover molecules of oxygen that are a direct result of using your brain.

Brain-derived neurotropic factor, usually referred to as BDNF, has been called Miracle-Gro for the brain (Medina, 2008; Ratey, 2008). It is released through exercise. By increasing neurotransmitter activity, improving blood flow, and producing brain-growth factors that act like fertilizer for the brain, exercise readies our neurons to connect more easily. Exercise performs this function better than any other factor of which we are currently aware.

Exercise has a number of other benefits. Specifically, it

• Improves attention and motivation by increasing levels of dopamine and norepinephrine.

- Decreases impulsivity by activating frontal lobe structures that inhibit random, divergent actions and thoughts through the release of more dopamine and serotonin.
- Creates more positive moods, lowers anxiety, and raises self-esteem through the release of more serotonin and norepinephrine.
- Helps overcome learned helplessness by improving resilience, improving self-confidence, and raising the ability to withstand stress and frustration.
- Causes stem cells in the brain to divide, which creates the possibility of making new brain cells.
- Adds new brain cells to the hippocampus (the memory control area), and may also add to the frontal cortex, where executive functioning takes place.
- Adds to the "chemical soup" that promotes the growth and survival of new neurons.

Exercise doesn't make you smarter, but it does make you able to focus and learn. Many schools are involved in studies to examine the link between exercise and learning. Naperville Central High School in Naperville, Illinois, is one of them. The school has developed a Zero Hour P.E. class, so named because it occurs in the morning before the school day begins. In these classes, sleepy students compete against themselves in physical fitness activities that raise their heart rates for a minimum of 25 minutes. The results have included higher test scores, better reading ability, and overall higher grades (Ratey, 2008).

In addition to its relationship to increased brain function, exercise is being examined for other purposes. Some studies indicate that attention deficit disorder (ADD) is better controlled through exercise than medication. Anxiety and depression are also affected by exercise, which may be more useful than other common methods of control. And, of course, the aging brain benefits from exercise in many ways, which may include a delay in the onset of dementia and Alzheimer's disease.

Does Art Make You Smart?

The question "Does art make you smart?" was recently answered by new research from a consortium of seven universities. Some of the foremost neuroscientists in the United States took part in the three-year collaboration, including Michael Gazzaniga from the University of California, Santa Barbara, Elizabeth Spelke of Harvard University, and Michael Posner of the University of Oregon. The consortium's findings "add new scientific support to the observation that children who participate in the arts also do well academically and suggest that changes in attention networks in the brain may be one reason" (Patoine, 2008). Although the research doesn't show a direct cause-and-effect relationship, it provides fuel for further study.

The brain's attention networks underlie one leading theory of how arts training influences cognition. According to this theory, children who are interested in an art form are motivated to practice; motivation "leads to sustained attention, which in turn leads to greater efficiency of the brain network involved in attention and to cognitive improvement" (Patoine, 2008).

To test the hypothesis, Posner developed a video game that would be interesting and motivating to children in the same way that arts training might be. Children 4 to 7 years old were tested for cognitive capacity before and after playing the game. The researchers also recorded electrical activity in the children's brains by placing electrodes on the scalp to determine whether patterns of activity in the attention networks changed as a result of the training. After five days of training with the video game, the children showed "clear evidence of improvements in the efficiency of a key attention network in the brain." According to Posner, "When you change that network, you also improve general cognitive capacity, as determined by intelligence tests." He concluded that the results of the study suggest that "absorbing a child in one of the art forms is one way to train the attentional network" (Patoine, 2008).

The consortium study uncovered some possible additional benefits of arts training, including the following:

• Music training has a positive relation to mathematics reasoning, particularly in geometry.

• Music training is closely correlated with improvements in reading fluency, reading attainment, and sequence learning.

• Music training and acting are associated with improvements in working memory.

• Learning to dance by watching others may be as effective as learning through physical movement; this observational learning may also transfer to other cognitive abilities.

Trial and Error: Who Learns from Mistakes?

Learning relies heavily on both positive and negative feedback. Positive feedback informs us to continue the pattern that is working. Negative feedback tells the brain that it's time to take a different approach. But learning from mistakes may be a developmental process. According to some research, our students don't necessarily learn from negative feedback at certain ages.

A study reported in the *Journal of Neuroscience* (van Duijvenvoorde et al., 2008) divided students into three age groups: 8- and 9-year-olds, 11- to 13-year-olds, and 18- to 25-year-olds. The researchers discovered that younger students do not benefit from negative feedback. This is not to say that they should be told that they are doing well when they are not. Rather, what appears to happen is that the negative feedback is not handled in their brains the way it is with older students. Before age 12, students will give up when receiving negative feedback or they will carry on incorrectly. It just doesn't seem to register that they need to make a change. In the study, the 8- and 9-year-olds' brains showed less activity in the area that monitors performance. By about age 12, the brain begins to respond differently. Negative feedback seems to affect the brain more, and more activity is seen as the brain monitors overall performance.

The results of the study suggest that we should give younger students more information in our negative feedback—for example, "That's not working well; why don't you try this?" The older students can simply be told "That's not working well," and, in terms of brain development, they should be able to figure out something different on their own.

So What?

The implications of this brain research are boundless. We now know that the brain is plastic, learns through observation, changes as a result of exercise, and is strengthened by the arts; we also know that different age levels respond to different types of feedback. What are we doing and what *should* we be doing to use this information to improve test scores and grades, increase student success, and help students develop their creativity, relationship skills, and ability to synthesize?

We should be carefully considering the technology available to our students and use it to motivate them, increase their attention, and enhance their learning. If educators model (for those mirror neurons) a balance between the use of high-tech equipment and communication devices on the one hand, and physical fitness and arts activities on the other, perhaps students will have even better brains.

TEXT MESSAGE

Find out how "balanced" your students are in terms of time spent using digital devices, exercising, and doing arts-related activities. Discuss with them the importance of each of these. Take this information to your administration and school board. Ask the following question: At what cost are we cutting programs that promote learning even though they may affect our students' ability to meet state standards? Remember, too, that most of the arts involve working with others and creating new ideas, two areas we want to enhance for the 21st century student.

CHAPTER 3

Do Brain-Based Principles Apply in the Digital Age?

Certain basic tenets about the brain can be applied in the classroom (Caine & Caine, 1994). In this chapter, we look at some of them, including the following:

- The brain needs multifaceted experiences.
- The brain seeks patterns.
- The brain searches for meaning.
- Stress inhibits learning.
- Learning is developmental.
- The brain is social.

The Brain Needs Multifaceted Experiences

According to James Zull (2002) in *The Art of Changing the Brain*, learning "is change in ourselves, because it is change in the brain" (p. xiv). To change on a long-term basis, the brain needs experiences that reinforce the changes that have occurred.

These experiences should reflect certain things that we know about learning, including the following:

- **Multisensory input**—Research strongly suggests that learning will be stronger and retrieval of information will be easier if more senses are involved.
- **Rewards and motivation**—Many students have very adaptive brains that will look for a way to get the reward without doing the work. Although extrinsic rewards can be worrisome, some rewards will motivate some students. If enjoyment of the learning ensues, then intrinsic motivation may take over.
- **Memory**—Without repetition, memories are difficult to recall. The amount of repetition required may depend on the amount of emotion attached to a specific memory. Experiences linked to emotion are easier to remember.
- **Prior knowledge**—Learning rarely occurs if it is not connected to something we already know.
- **From concrete to abstract**—Because the frontal lobe, the area of the brain where abstract thinking occurs, is slow to develop, it behooves us to begin with concrete examples and then move to the abstract. Even older students may have trouble jumping directly into abstractions.
- **Practice**—Practice makes permanent. Therefore, we must be certain that our students are not practicing misconceptions. First, they must be able to talk and write about a concept or skill so we can be aware of their understanding.
- **Stories**—Stories engage many areas of the brain. They come from our experiences, our memories, our ideas, our actions, and our feelings. Because stories have beginnings, middles, and endings, they help to develop the sequencing and organizing processes of the brain. Stories also engage many different emotional triggers that are helpful in retrieving information.
- **Computers and other forms of technology**—Many senses are engaged when students work together doing assignments and research on a computer. The work is visual, auditory, and kinesthetic. It also involves interacting with others.

The Brain Seeks Patterns

The information stored in our brains is stored as patterns. As we watch someone write a word, our brain starts retrieving words that might fit the pattern. It is engaging, and it calls for immediate connections. For instance, consider this sequence:

FA (What word could this be? *Farm*? *Fat*? *Fall*?)

FAT (Hmm. Another letter causes my brain to look for other patterns. *Fathom*? *Father*?)

FATH (Now I'm sure it's either *father* or *fathom*. Am I correct?)

FATHEAD (That's a good thing—our brains need fat to function properly!)

This is how the brain works. Information must make sense to the brain or it will be dropped. In fact, 99 percent of incoming information is dropped. Given the quantity of messages bombarding the brain, anything that is not familiar, does not make sense, or is not associated with survival may be quickly disposed of.

Daniel Pink (2005) believes that the current era calls for a way of thinking that he calls "high concept," which includes the capacity to detect patterns and create something new. The only way to detect patterns is to have them stored in the brain. It is imperative that educators take new information, help students "see" the patterns, associate those patterns with older patterns stored in the brain, and create new ones.

According to Judy Willis (2006), patterns are passageways for memories to follow. What can we do to set up these passageways? The two most effective ways to help students see patterns are graphic organizers and chunking information.

Graphic Organizers

Graphic organizers help students create a visual version of their learning. They come in many forms. I have devoted an entire chapter in this book to the topic of mind maps because they are a very brain-compatible form of graphic organizer and offer students an opportunity to make some choices and be creative (see Chapter 9). Other common graphic organizers include Venn diagrams, T charts, KWHL charts, and sequence charts (see Figure 3.1). Creating these on a program such as Inspiration may be fun for students.

Figure 3.1	Graphic Organizers

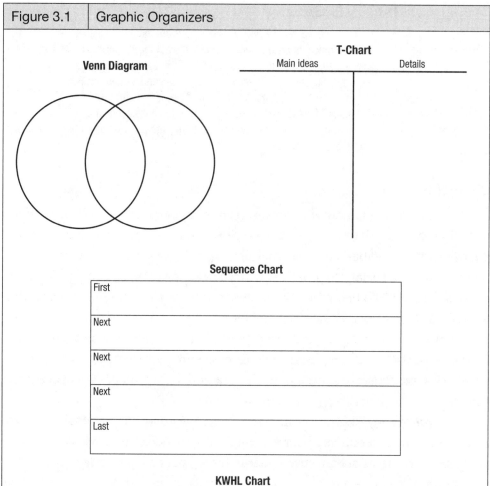

Venn Diagram

T-Chart

Main ideas   Details

Sequence Chart

First

Next

Next

Next

Last

KWHL Chart

K	W	H	L
What do we know?	What do we want to find out?	How can we find out what we want to learn?	What did we learn?

INSTANT MESSAGE

Some schools choose a few graphic organizers that every teacher uses, so students become accustomed to what the organizers are asking them to look for. The skill of filling out these schoolwide learning tools becomes stored in students' procedural memory. For instance, after using Venn diagrams to compare and contrast information in different classrooms, students automatically begin looking for similarities and differences when they are given or asked to create a Venn diagram.

Chunking

"Chunking" is a common way to organize information. As students learn to read, they chunk together sounds, letters, and words to make the reading meaningful. Phone numbers and credit card numbers are typically chunked. Both types of numbers are usually chunked in groups of three or four. When you encounter a phone number (or other familiar grouping) that is chunked differently than the way you are used to, it can be much harder to remember.

Chunking is what many educators do to condense the enormous amount of curriculum material that is supposed to be covered into a manageable amount. When a teacher says, "There are three points I want you to remember," we can assume that those three points cover a lot of material.

When written or verbal information is chunked effectively, it is logical, organized, and consistent. This enhances your students' ability to understand what is going on. Written material that is chunked and hierarchical gives readers quick access to the big picture. From there they can get into the details as needed. And a verbal format that is well structured and logically chunked helps listeners follow and remember key ideas or details as necessary. Chunking is a lot like filing. You want to open only one "file" at a time, so that you can stay focused and "file" the information easily. This process will save time, and it will also help your students understand better and remember more effectively.

The Brain Searches for Meaning

Just as the brain seeks patterns, it also searches for meaning, especially personal meaning. What is meaningful to our students may be very different from what is meaningful to us. Because the brain wants to learn (and, in fact, those dendrites are always moving and looking for new information), it will try to make sense of new information and will find that information more meaningful if it relates to personal life.

Relational memory occurs when students can relate new learning to something that has happened previously in their lives. Adding to patterns or maps previously stored and mastered makes learning much easier (Willis, 2006).

The Net Generation, more than any other, will be coteachers in the classroom. It has always been important for students to become teachers in order to increase their memory of content, but today we have students who are quite capable of changing the way we look at education. Their facility with research, their unique ability to scan Web pages in seconds, and their superb use of tools to get the job done puts them in a league of their own. They are unafraid of the discovery process if they can use the equipment that has become part of their daily lives.

These students insist on finding meaning and having fun. They have the ability to show us the way. Even our young students will show us their needs and their ways of connecting to curriculum. Some of these children may not be as experienced with computers and iPods as others, but they may be skilled at photography and other forms of visuals. We must be careful observers of our classrooms and look for opportunities to make curriculum more meaningful.

Parent involvement may be a key to making curriculum meaningful. Providing topics for discussion at home and key questions may encourage family connections to content.

If the brain finds no meaning in information, it will drop it. What kinds of behaviors will we see in students who don't "get it?" According to Rogers (2008), we will see an "I don't care" attitude because it is better to look like you don't care rather than to look like you don't understand. Heads down on desks is something we have all seen. If a student attempts to distract your teaching, it may be because the brain is putting a stop to whatever is making it feel inferior. Therefore, the student who is most disruptive is probably the student having the most difficulty.

How can we help students find meaning in what we are teaching? One possibility is the use of a different graphic organizer, one I label KWHLU. It is just like the KWHL chart in Figure 3.1 (see p. 29), but adds one more column for the student to fill in after the learning has taken place. The *U* is for "How can I *use* this information in my life?" This puts a bit of responsibility on the students and is useful if the students are motivated enough to do the learning without knowing initially how it will relate to their life.

Another way to help students find meaning is through storytelling. This strategy may involve students listening to other students' stories. Perhaps through another's personal connection, students will find their own. When students have stories to tell about content, it is important to give them the opportunity to share. This approach helps both the storyteller and the listeners. If there are too many stories to share with the whole class, divide the students into groups and have them tell their stories to small groups of classmates.

Get to know your students' world. This may involve watching MTV, listening to popular music stations, attending extracurricular events, eavesdropping carefully on some conversations, being aware of the latest fashion trends, and checking out where students hang out. The more you know about your students' world, the easier it will be to relate what you want them to know in a meaningful way.

Guest speakers and field trips will also be helpful. You and your students can make meaning together by having the same experiences. Give them a chance to personally relate these experiences to their lives or to school.

The World Wide Web offers innumerable ways to make meaning. By exploring any topic, students can search for information that is meaningful to them on various Web sites.

Giving students choices is another useful approach. For example, one of your science or math learning standards may be "Collect, organize, and analyze data." Is it necessary for all students to use the same data? One 7th grade teacher gave students choices related to the following inquiries that required collecting, organizing, and analyzing data:

- Will there be a white Christmas?
- How many M&Ms of each color are found in a bag?
- What is the drink of choice among students in your grade?

Stress Inhibits Learning

It's the first day of "the test." The teachers have been talking about it for weeks. The students have been pretested and retested. The school cheerleaders made up a cheer about the test, and the school held a special pep assembly to cheer for the students and encourage them to get good scores. Exercises to develop test-taking skills have been repeated many times. No one knows for sure who is more stressed over the test, the teachers or the students.

To be certain that the students' brains are nourished, special snacks are served the week of the test. Some schools offer healthy protein snacks, some provide fruits and vegetables, and some think doughnuts will do the trick. The students are offered bribes: "If the class does well on the test, we'll have a picnic." (Most schools' test scores are not available until school is out, so I'm not sure how they follow up on this one.)

The pressure is on. Teachers pass out the test booklets. They read the instructions exactly as they are written in the teacher's manual. They pick up their stopwatches and say, "Begin!"

Some of the students are completely unimpressed by the efforts of the school to get them to perform better. They simply read through the test at their own pace or, in some cases, fill in the blanks without reading the test. These students feel no stress.

Some other students are in a "good stress" situation. The adrenaline and cortisol running through their bodies doesn't put them in the stress-response mode. Instead, these hormones prime them for reading, understanding, making connections, and synthesizing information to help them provide the correct answers for the test.

Then there are some students who are overwhelmed by testing in general or who are so pumped up by the emphasis put on this test that as soon as they enter the classroom their hearts start racing, their respiration becomes more rapid, their mouths become dry, and they experience a full-fledged stress response. When the teacher says "Begin!" and they open their booklets, it seems as though their brains stop working. What they are experiencing is a fight-or-flight response, which causes blood to flow to the hands or the legs, readying the body to fight or flee. The blood is not in the brain where it is needed. Some of these students are resilient enough to overcome this stress. It may take a few minutes and some deep breaths, but they are able to calm themselves and allow blood flow to return to the brain. Others are not so lucky. Some students with test anxiety need some special tools to help them overcome it. The question is have the school and the teacher caused the anxiety?

We all know that some students enter our classrooms already stressed. A number of them have very stressful personal lives. A few have difficulty with social interactions with their peers on the bus or the playground. And then there are those who are stressed by school. Perhaps they don't do well academically or don't fit into any social group.

Providing an Environment That Lessens Stress

Lowering stress requires finding a comfort level in the environment and with the people in that environment. Environmental factors that may lower stress include the following:

• A feeling of belonging is established through group work in which input is valued by the group and by the teacher.

• Students have specific tasks they must perform every day for the good of the classroom, such as emptying the pencil sharpener or taking attendance. These chores change periodically so all students can experience doing different ones.

• Procedures are in place and may be posted where students can see them every day. Students have learned the procedures that they will need to follow regularly. They know what to do and how to do it.

• Lesson previews or agendas are posted in the same spot every day. The teacher reads these to the students or has students read them out loud.

• Rules and consequences are consistent. The teacher models what is expected of the students.

• Clear targets are posted and discussed. Students know what the goal of the lesson is and can share that information with others.

- Students are taught how their brains work and realize what they need to help them learn and succeed.
- Music is part of the classroom environment (see Chapter 8).
- Technology is available in the classroom for those digital natives who feel comfortable with it.

Lowering stress increases learning. Stressed brains don't learn in the same way as brains that aren't stressed. Students who feel they excel in an area at school will feel better about themselves, and their brains will release chemicals that make them feel good, like dopamine and serotonin, rather than the stress chemical cortisol.

Using Rituals to Lessen Stress

Every Christmas you go to Grandma's house. While you are there, Uncle Sam always gives a toast before Christmas Eve dinner. After dinner you go to church. The day after Christmas all the females in the family go shopping.

Which of these are *rituals*, and which are *routines*? You may think it doesn't make any difference, but it can. A routine is something you do regularly. A ritual is a prescribed method of eliciting a specific *response*. Going to dinner and shopping are routines that are performed on a regular basis. Uncle Sam's toast and going to church are rituals that elicit specific feelings or brain states from the participants.

Why is this important? Establishing rituals in your classroom is a very powerful way to reduce stress, to manage your classroom, and to encourage the acquisition of knowledge. Authors Eric Jensen and Harry Wong highly recommend using procedures and rituals to enhance classroom management. Eric told me that I needed to have 25 to 35 rituals in place as soon as possible. What's that you say? Impossible? Let's look at a few minutes of a typical day in my classroom:

> At 8:15 the first bell rings. As the students walk down the hall to enter my room, I am standing at the door. I greet each student with a handshake or high-five and a "Good morning, _____!" The CD player is playing morning songs; this year I am using some Beatles songs. At 8:25 I walk over to the player and stop the CD. The students go to their seats and quiet down. I then take attendance and lunch count. We always discuss the menu for the day because we like to get as many hot-lunch people as possible in order to break old records. I then say, "Please, stand up" and we say the Pledge of Allegiance. I turn the morning music back on while the children wait for the 8:30 bell.

When the 8:30 bell rings, I signal to the students that they may go to their first class. The students file out as I stand at the door to greet the next class. As soon as this class has entered, I go to the CD player and turn off the music. The students go directly to their seats and wait for my statement: "If you have 100 percent of your team members seated and ready to go, raise your hand and say yes!" The students comply and answer. In this way I can quickly ascertain who is present.

In just 15 minutes there were a minimum of eight rituals. Each of these served the purpose of putting those students into specific states. The classroom is managed without saying anything specifically related to management. The students simply respond to the rituals.

Why do rituals work? They provide a sense of safety and security. Brain research tells us that a feeling of safety provides the opportunity for information to move up to the cerebral cortex, where higher-order thinking takes place. Students become accustomed to the use of rituals, and the consistency allows them to feel safe and secure in your classroom. Does this mean you can never do anything out of the ordinary? Absolutely not. On the contrary, rituals allow you to do things that you might otherwise not be able to do.

Learning Is Developmental

As the brain grows and develops, it is ready for different types of learning. This principle applied in the industrial age and the information age, and it applies today in the digital age, or the so-called conceptual age. The brain will not be fully developed until the mid-20s, and it will follow developmental stages that may coincide with certain age ranges. However, each brain develops at its own pace.

The following sections highlight major developments in the brain at various ages. See Appendix A on pp. 151–160 for information about the parts of the brain and the various processes referred to in these sections.

Ages 2 Through 4

• Between the ages of 2 and 3, pruning of synapses begins. Neural pathways that are used are kept and those that are not begin to disappear.

• At around age 3, language explodes, episodic memory emerges, and the corpus callosum connects the two sides of the frontal lobes, improving thinking, language, and emotional skills.

• At around age 4, neurons aiding long-term memory emerge, math areas begin to develop in the parietal lobe, and gains are seen in visual-motor coordination as myelination and lobe growth continue.

Ages 5 Through 7

• Myelination of the corpus callosum of the frontal lobe continues, leading to more cross-talk between hemispheres.

• Dendritic complexity increases to facilitate the formation of memory. Electrical activity of the brain gains "coherence," allowing the brain to better integrate the past with the present.

• Memory strategies begin to develop.

• Improving connections between the temporal and parietal lobes lead to dramatic development of reading and vocabulary skills.

• At age 6, dopamine levels in the prefrontal cortex are nearly the same as in an adult, allowing improved focus and concentration.

• At age 7, synaptic density in the frontal lobes peaks, and pathways between the frontal lobes and the limbic system lead to better impulse control, greater independence, improved planning ability, and acceptance of responsibility.

• Also at age 7, growth in the Broca's area allows children to begin to understand things like irony and sarcasm (Sprenger, 2008).

Ages 8 Through 10

• Accelerated growth of the prefrontal cortex begins at age 8, leading to more impulse control and abstract thinking (Kagan & Herschkowitz, 2005).

• Organization for memory begins around age 8.

• From ages 8 to 9, children learn best through positive feedback due to the development of their cognitive control center; negative feedback, or learning from one's mistakes, remains a challenge (van Duijvenvoorde et al., 2008).

• The brain strengthens its ability to learn as myelination of fibers speeds associations between senses and ideas.

• Children in this age group are no longer learning to read, but are reading to learn (Healy, 2004).

Ages 11 Through 13

• By age 11, children begin to manipulate abstract ideas.
• By age 12, growth of the cognitive control center allows children to learn from negative feedback—that is, to learn from their mistakes (van Duijven-voorde et al., 2008).
• While the first 10 years of life are dedicated to the development of sensory lobes, the second 10 years show great development of executive functions in the frontal lobe.

Ages 14 Through 18

• More pruning of frontal lobes occurs as students "design" their own brain; as the brain matures, it is capable of better abstract reasoning.
• Working memory increases throughout the teen years.

Technology and Brain Development

The American Association of Pediatrics announced in 2001 that children under the age of 2 should spend no time before a computer or television screen. Their time should be spent interacting with others as they move more and listen to and participate in conversation. From ages 3 to 5, it is recommended that television be limited to no more than two hours per day (Committee on Public Education, 2001).

The Net Generation of young adults with children is not necessarily following these suggestions. Babies are sitting on laps learning how to hit keys and move a mouse to become computer literate. Two experts, Jane Healy (1998) and Susan Greenfield (2008), agree that children should not be exposed to technology until they are older. Healy suggests children should be at least 7 years old before they use computers.

We must remember that brain growth occurs through movement and play. We should also remind ourselves that interaction with others is necessary for brain growth. The Net Geners must work together with their technology to create that balance between the real world and the cyber world.

The Brain Is Social

As you read in Chapter 1, social interaction can be a troublesome area for the digital natives. It's not that they are antisocial; rather, physical interaction with others is deferred because of the time they spend with technology.

One of the components of social intelligence as described by Goleman (2006) is social cognition—simply understanding how the social world works. In a classroom, this ability might include the following components:

- Recognizing different social groups or cliques
- Knowing classmates' close friends
- Knowing how to make friends
- Knowing how to show empathy
- Having the ability to listen
- Knowing when and how to show emotions
- Recognizing an emotion being expressed facially and with gestures

Teaching students social cognition requires helping them develop relationships in which to practice being a social person. The team approach described in Chapter 5 may be helpful. Other possibilities are flexible grouping, pairing students, role playing, and discussing events that your students may have seen on television in regard to social interactions and behavior.

A point to remember about emotions is that they are contagious (Goleman, 2006). The fact that the brain adjusts itself to match the brains in its surroundings is amazing. We tend to smile when someone smiles at us. A reaction by mirror neurons causes this, but sometimes just the act of smiling makes us happy.

From the Dark Ages to the Digital Age

It's time for educators to join this unbelievably fast-paced digital age. The principles of brain research still apply, and technology enhances our ability to help students' brains grow. Although some of us digital dinosaurs may not feel that technology is compatible with our brains, it is compatible with our students' brains. Their brains have adapted quite well to the high-tech world, and although some of the brain changes have negative consequences, if we stay on top of things we can help our students succeed in today's world.

TEXT MESSAGE

 There are other brain-based teaching principles that I did not include in this chapter. One of them is "each brain is unique." I believe the scope of this book reinforces this principle. Our students' brains are changing according to their experiences, and technology has become a large part of the daily life experiences of many of our students.

PART 2

Desk Space, MySpace, My Style

The classroom has changed. It now encompasses interacting with information and people all over the world. Students need to find a balance between cyberspace and personal interactions with their peers and their teachers. In Part 2 we look at learning environments that meet the needs of the whole child, setting up teams to get students working together, and understanding learning styles and multiple intelligences.

CHAPTER 4

Environments for Learning

The kinds of demands our students will face in the 21st century require that we provide many different kinds of learning environments. The traditional classroom is changing. Students are no longer confined to the space within four walls. Getting connected to each other is one aspect of the change. But beyond that, students can connect with people other than their classmates through Skype, MySpace, blogs, and wikis. This interaction is one of the benefits of the digital world. Students can both learn and teach in this world. Education is available everywhere.

Despite the changes that this new world presents, certain important elements of an effective learning environment remain the same. These include a need for safety and security, opportunities for working with others, having adequate time to complete work, being offered choices, and engaging with a curriculum that is relevant. Both high-tech and low-tech brains respond to these things in a positive way, and they are part of educating the whole child.

A brain-compatible environment that embraces the whole child must be predictable as well as novel; learning requires both. Although that sounds like an oxymoron, to the brain, it is not. As discussed in earlier chapters, the brain is attracted to novelty. But without the security provided by predictability, the brain's response to novelty is to flee or fight. Predictability creates the sense of safety and security that allows information to be accessed by the brain.

As we consider the elements of a brain-compatible environment in this digital age, we can use the following tenets set forth in the compact developed by the Commission on the Whole Child (2007) as a guide:

- Each student enters school healthy and learns about and practices a healthy lifestyle.
- Each student learns in an intellectually challenging environment that is physically and emotionally safe for students and adults.
- Each student is actively engaged in learning and is connected to the school and broader community.
- Each graduate is prepared for success in college or further study and for employment in a global environment.
- Each student has access to personalized learning and is supported by qualified, caring adults.

The following sections discuss each of these in detail.

Encouraging Healthy Lifestyles

Brain-compatible teachers teach their students about the brain. It is important for every child to understand the structure of the brain, the functions of various parts of the brain, and the brain-body connection.

Sleep is one factor that illustrates the brain-body connection. Students should know about the amount of sleep they need because it is a crucial factor in their ability to learn, remember, and be successful. According to one study, the loss of one to one-and-a-half hours of nighttime sleep can reduce daytime alertness by one-third (Bonnet & Arand, 1995). Inadequate sleep raises stress levels, and as much as teachers try to create low-stress environments, sleep-deprived students will enter the classroom with higher levels of stress hormones.

Furthermore, the amounts of these hormones will increase throughout the day as students become frustrated as a result of failures to understand content and misunderstandings with others. Figure 4.1 shows recommended amounts of sleep for various ages.

Figure 4.1	Recommended Hours of Sleep for Children
Ages	**Recommended Duration of Sleep**
Preschool	11–13 hours
5–10	10–11 hours
11–17	9 hours, 15 minutes
18 and above	8 hours

Nutrition is another factor in having a healthy body, brain, and lifestyle. Many of our students start the school day with no breakfast or with inappropriate choices for their first meal of the day. They need to know that the brain is the only organ that cannot store energy; therefore, coming to school without breakfast leaves the brain running on empty. The brain burns 20 to 25 percent of our daily caloric intake, and it is vital to put healthy foods into our bodies. Students need to know how to make better choices when it comes to food. They need to learn what their bodies and brains need. The food pyramid offered by the United States Department of Agriculture can be downloaded and given to students or posted on a bulletin board as a reminder of what good nutrition consists of. It can be found at www.mypyramid.gov/pyramid/index.html. This site offers suggestions for the basic food groups and has interactive tools to plan and keep track of food intake. The Net Generation may find the interactivity of the food pyramid site motivational as well as educational.

Exercise is also an important part of a healthy lifestyle. Students need to be aware of what exercise will do for their bodies and their brains. Recent research presented by John Ratey (2008) in his book *Spark: The Revolutionary New Science of Exercise and the Brain* convinces us that proper exercise as part of a daily or weekly routine will raise achievement. With this in mind, some schools are replacing chairs with exercise balls for students to sit or bounce on while they learn. Teachers are allowing students to stand and fidget during lessons, and some chairs in classrooms have swinging footrests. John Medina also has information about exercise on his Web site, www.brainrules.net.

INSTANT MESSAGE

 Climate control can contribute to having a healthy place to learn. Although installing climate control devices may involve making expensive changes in some schools, the research suggests that students learn best when the temperature is between 68°F and 72°F degrees.

Providing a Safe and Intellectually Challenging Environment

Every student deserves to feel safe and secure in school. Feeling safe and secure lowers stress levels and opens up the brain's filters—the reticular activating system, located in the brain stem; and the amygdala, found in the limbic area of the brain (Willis, 2006). Information processing cannot take place unless incoming information is allowed to enter the brain and eventually enter the neocortex for higher-level thinking and for storage.

A total absence of stress is unlikely in any environment, but a brain-compatible teacher provides a classroom where stress is low and threat is almost nonexistent. As discussed in Chapter 3, things teachers can do to reduce stress include establishing and posting frequently used procedures, posting lesson previews or agendas, establishing and modeling consistent rules and consequences, and posting and discussing clear targets for lessons.

Engaging in Learning and Connecting to the School and Broader Community

Actively engaging students in their learning depends on arousing their interest, and interest, in turn, often depends on the choices they are given and how meaningful the curriculum is to them. In addition, formative assessments and informational feedback, flexible grouping patterns, and connections to the world outside the classroom can help keep them motivated and engaged.

Choice

Choice changes behavior, motivates, provides a sense of ownership, and makes the world seem right to the learner. Choice is also the key to differentiating instruction in the classroom (Nunley, 2007). Students can be offered choices in how they want to study content, what area of content they wish to pursue, and how they present what they know.

Classroom management can rely on choice as well. When students are distracting others but not breaking a specific rule, offering a choice often puts them back on track. For instance, when one very kinesthetic learner, Nick, began to slink back in his seat and put his long legs in the aisle in hopes of tripping a fellow classmate, his teacher wisely offered him a choice. "Nick, I could really use those long legs of yours. I have several articles that need to be added to the bulletin board. You could either put them up for me while you listen to the lecture, or you may draw a mind map of this lecture to put up on the bulletin board later." Nick realized he had just missed getting into trouble, and he was pleased that he could now do one of two things that he enjoyed. His teacher redirected his attention back on the topic in less than a minute and was able to continue her lesson.

In addition to its role in day-to-day instruction and management, choice can play a role in long-term projects. Students' reluctance to do class projects often stems from the choices we are offering them. Some teachers offer no choice, whereas others offer only a few. It is true that each project requires an assessment, and making many rubrics to assess each individual project can be very time consuming. But brain-compatible teachers can offer students the opportunity to create their own rubrics to match the projects. Some students may create their rubrics from templates available on many Web sites. By offering students the choice of how to create the rubrics, a feeling of control and ownership is further enhanced, and using a rubric helps students see connections between what they are supposed to be learning and how they will show that they are actually learning. Teachers can review the rubrics and give the final OK on their use.

Project choices may be based on various considerations, such as learning styles, multiple intelligences, and interests. Asking students to make lists of possible products ensures that almost every student will find something appealing. A brainstorming session can bring forth many good suggestions from students.

Providing choice scares some teachers, because they believe they might lose control of the situation. In fact, they gain a great deal of influence with their students, and discipline is rarely a problem.

If classroom or schoolwide rules and agendas are in place, choice points may be limited but still possible. For instance, lunch scheduled for 11:30 a.m. leaves no room for choice, but how the students line up for lunch is an area for choice. The school schedule may require reading at 9:30 a.m., but students might choose whether to read alone, in groups, in pairs, with a tape recorder or an iPod, or on the computer.

Meaningful Curriculum

As discussed in Chapter 3, Net Geners have an unprecedented opportunity to teach as well as learn in the classroom because of their ability to conduct online research, use digital tools, and scan Web pages in seconds. Discovery is an important part of their everyday lives. Observing their world and what they are interested in is key to providing curriculum and lessons that are meaningful to them. Involving parents by providing topics for home discussion is another way to connect with students' lives outside of school.

Formative Assessment with Timely Feedback

Some people believe that we don't assess enough. Ask most teachers and they'll say we assess too much. But are we all talking about the same thing? The form of assessment that causes much stress and appears to be taking over more time than necessary in some schools is *summative* assessment. It includes chapter and unit tests, end-of-year tests, and standardized tests. In the words of Rick Stiggins (2001), this is assessment "of" learning.

Formative assessment is a process used by teachers and students before, during, and after instruction that provides feedback to adjust ongoing teaching and learning to improve student achievement. Black and Wiliam (1998) provide strong evidence from an extensive literature review to show that classroom formative assessment, properly implemented, is a powerful means to improve student learning—but summative assessments such as standardized exams can have a harmful effect.

Because metaphors are memorable, I like to compare assessment and cooking. Formative assessment occurs when the cook tastes the food before serving the guests. Summative assessment occurs when the guests taste the food. If you were cooking for others and found the food distasteful, you could throw it out and try something new, add some things to change the flavor, or order in from a restaurant. Formative assessment gives teachers the information they need to change their students' outcomes by throwing out the current approach in use, adding or changing some of the lessons, or bringing in a new approach like another teacher, a guest speaker, or a computer program.

Formative assessment is ongoing, so students can receive feedback about their progress in a timely manner. How important is this? After looking at more than 7,000 studies, John Hattie and Helen Timperley (2007) concluded that providing students with specifics about how they are doing in regard to the learning objectives raised student achievement 37 percentile points!

Simple ways to find out if your students understand what you are teaching are easily available. Providing them with colored disks, cups, or markers can give you information. After offering part of a lesson, or even while you are delivering information, students may hold up a red cup that tells you "Stop! I don't get it." A yellow cup tells you to slow down, and a green cup gives you the go-ahead. This simple method is a great way to differentiate your teaching because in moments you may find out where each student is in the learning process.

Exit cards are another form of quick assessment. Although waiting until the end of class may be gathering information somewhat late, according to Dylan Wiliam (2008), this simple process offers you a bit more information than the colored cups. On an exit card (which could also be an "entrance card" or a "mid-class card"), students write down three things they understand, two questions they may have, and one piece of information they can connect to some prior knowledge. Figure 4.2 (see p. 50) provides some other examples of exit cards. After collecting the cards, you can divide them into two or three groups: Group 1 understands the material and can be grouped to work more extensively on the concept; Group 2 almost gets it and can work in a small-group format to discuss it further; Group 3 doesn't really get it and requires reteaching.

Figure 4.2	Examples of Exit Cards
Exit Card #1 1. Name three things you have learned in class today. 2. Write one vocabulary word and define it.	**Exit Card #2** 1. Explain the difference between a simile and a metaphor. 2. Write an example of each.
Exit Card #3 1. Explain the difference between prime and composite numbers. 2. Give examples of each.	**Exit Card #4** 1. Write a sentence that contains two prepositional phrases. 2. Underline the phrases and circle the object of each phrase.

The brain needs to know what to focus on, what to pay attention to, and how to frame the learning—and feedback can help with all three. In this digital age, students can keep track of their accomplishments through computer programs, on blogs, or on their iPods. If you are looking for ways to give the Net Generation feedback, you have some interesting options. Send them text messages: it's personal, prompt, and they can't resist reading them! Add comments to their blogs. If they are working online, instant messaging is a fast way to connect.

Flexible Grouping

To develop brains that are able to create, synthesize, and relate to others in a respectful, empathic way, students must engage in both small and large groups. Classroom and school environments need to expose students to many kinds of situations for interaction. Research suggests that cooperative learning increases student achievement (Marzano, Pickering, & Pollack, 2001). Anecdotal evidence suggests that students are happier, more comfortable, and achieve more when they know and like their classmates, and grouping provides the setting to encourage such feelings. Brains learn best when working with other brains. More learning takes place when students are working on computers together.

In Chapter 5, you will read about building strong classroom teams that work together, get to know each other, and support each other. Although creating teams is one way of grouping students, throughout the course of a day or a unit flexible grouping is imperative. Changing needs, levels of readiness, interests, and learning styles should all be considered when grouping.

After whole-class instruction, teachers may divide students into small groups. They may first use a think-pair-share activity in which students think about the topic or a guiding question, find a partner, and share their thoughts or feelings. This may precede another group activity constructed by simply putting pairs in groups of four. These temporary groups may work together for minutes, days, or weeks.

Flexible grouping enhances learning by doing the following:

- Giving students the opportunity to work with a variety of people
- Allowing students to explore material in different ways
- Permitting students to share work and responsibility
- Allowing students' ideas to be heard and valued

Class meetings can contribute to a brain-compatible environment. These may be scheduled regularly or on an as-needed basis. I have found that regularly scheduled meetings help build structure into the school week, but many "emergency" meetings need to be held as well.

Connecting Beyond the Classroom

Years ago I would have questioned the validity of students connecting to other classrooms in their buildings or classrooms anywhere in the world via technology. I knew the value of face-to-face contact and, the need for emotional literacy. We've come a long way. The opportunities are too great, the desire too strong. Teachers are recognizing this connectedness, and it's working on many levels.

In their article "The Joy of Blogging," Davis and McGrail (2009) describe their blogging experiment with 5th grade students in Georgia. The project was intended to help improve communication skills. The students' blogs could be read by anyone, and they received feedback from around the world.

Digital media are an obvious way for teachers and schools to connect with parents and for students to connect to the larger community, but that doesn't necessarily have to be the format you choose. Try these suggestions for connecting with students' families:

- Phone each family at the beginning of the school year. Create a relationship with family members before there are any problems with their student. Then if you have to call with an issue, they will be more receptive to you.
- Phone when a child is absent for more than a day. Let your students know that they are missed.
- Send home a newsletter once a week, twice a month, or just monthly. If your classroom has a Web site or a blog, post classroom news there.

Here are some suggestions for connecting students with the larger community:

- Investigate possibilities for your class to do a community service project.
- Bring in guest speakers from various areas of the community. Possibilities include public library personnel, government officials, and retail shop owners.
- Give your students the opportunity to share their digital expertise with businesses that may be interested in using some creative technology.

Preparing for College, Further Study, and Work in a Global Environment

We strive to teach students content through standards and goals. We let test results on those standards drive education. At the same time, we must remember that our students will be living in a far different world than what we know today. Preparing them for an unknown future is frightening, but nevertheless, that is what we are doing. According to modern medicine and the futurists, our students will be living for another 100 years. We don't know what content they will need to know. We do know that we must prepare them to be flexible, to take on challenges, and to shift their skills and expectations as needed.

Norms for the Net Generation, as described by Tapscott (2009), are characterized by these eight rules:

1. A need for speed—They are accustomed to real-time interactions on a global level.

2. Freedom of choice and expression—Those drop-down menus have been offering them choices for years; they expect to have choices.

3. Corporate integrity and openness—They get all the answers before they decide where to work and what to purchase.

4. Entertainment and play—They expect that school, work, and social interactions will include these elements.

5. Collaboration and relationships—Through their networking, they find out what others are using and doing to gather data; they communicate quickly with friends, colleagues, and employers and expect quick responses.

6. Customization and personalization—They have been able to interact and exchange ideas; they can change the content on certain Web sites; they personalize their work. Wikipedia is an example.

7. Scrutiny—They look carefully and are aware of their market power; they will scrutinize the company they work for, as well as others.

8. Innovation—They desire what is new and what gives them more groundbreaking features; they expect innovation in their workplace and want novel ways to collaborate, work, and learn.

Preparing students for the 21st century requires taking these characteristics into consideration. In the classroom, they need opportunities to share their expertise. Respect their digital brains and recognize that they can teach us and each other. Their digital expertise is an important part of their world and their future. Give them time to figure out how their easy accessibility to information can be used to help them make decisions, evaluate, synthesize, and create something new. Consider the following examples:

Henry is the Twitter king in his middle school. Sasha's blog is followed by almost every girl in class. Wikis (Web sites where users can add or edit content) are Edgar's claim to fame. These are just three of many students who have a passion and a skill for using digital media. Give them and others the opportunity to share what they know. Then give your class an opportunity to brainstorm ways to use these tools to enhance their learning experience. When Edgar was given the chance to show his classmates how to set up wiki pages, one of his examples was Wikipedia, the online interactive encyclopedia. He took his classmates to the site and to the topic "causes of earthquakes," where he showed them the articles, the log-in requirements if they wished to edit the page, and how to edit the entry. He was very specific about the issue of integrity when adding information to a wiki. This was an opportunity to add to a body of knowledge to make it better, not a license to mislead others. Most of his classmates had used Wikipedia, but they hadn't realized how interactive this site was, nor how to add to it. The class then discussed how they could set up wikis about the content areas they were studying. Edgar's expertise and interest was respected, and the entire class learned from this experience. Future lessons included "Blogging Like a Pro" by Sasha and "Add Twittering to Your Life" by Henry. Soon many students stepped up to give lessons in other areas or to present how they had applied the new skills learned from their classmates' lessons.

Access to Personalized Learning and Support from Qualified, Caring Adults

Many schools still follow a one-size-fits-all approach to learning. Despite the research that suggests a differentiated or personalized approach to instruction will increase student learning, the structure of our educational system makes it difficult for many teachers to embrace a whole-child experience. Schools leaders who recognize that students learn in different ways have reaped the benefits. (Gardner, 2006; Sternberg, 1996; Tomlinson, 1999) But change is slow and difficult; and moving from a traditional approach to an individualized, whole-child approach represents a dramatic shift. Castleman and Littky (2007) offer several suggestions:

- Find people in your school or community interested in supporting the whole child.
- Offer students the opportunity to explore their interests in the real world.
- Create advisory groups that meet weekly with the same students and advisor throughout high school.
- Let students have a voice in their choice of study.

Personalized learning may also include internships and mentoring programs, online classes, and classes at local colleges. There is no definition of an appropriate learning environment that will work for all students.

Ensuring that students have qualified, caring adults in their lives is another important factor in their success. It would be ideal if all parents fit the example of a qualified, caring adult. Those students who have parents involved in their education have a better chance at succeeding in school, but whether adult support comes from within the family or from an outside source, students can succeed.

According to Deborah Stipek (2006), "When students have a secure relationship with their teachers, they are more comfortable taking risks that enhance learning—tackling challenging tasks, persisting when they run into difficulty, or asking questions when they are confused" (p. 46).

If students are interested in a particular career, find people in your community who work in that field. See if you can set up a mentoring program between your students and some of the community members. For example, if a small number of your students are interested in health care, you may be able to find a medical facility that is willing to have students visit, help, and learn.

It takes only one special person to make a difference in a student's life. Perhaps that person is not you; but it behooves you to find counselors, support staff, or other teachers who connect with the student and can form a bond throughout the student's school career.

A Learning Environment for the 21st Century

Just as the definition of a family has changed over the years, the definition of an effective learning environment has changed as well. Of course, some components are the same: students need to learn in safe, healthy environments where they are encouraged and good modeling is on display. But educators need to become more aware of students' needs and interests so teachers can help them devise an education plan that will be motivating and will sustain them through challenges, frustrations, and successes.

We must all keep in mind that the learning environment should be flexible. Students need opportunities to work with their peers, their teachers, and community members who may be interested in preparing the whole child for the 21st century.

TEXT MESSAGE

Here are some suggestions for help in creating a learning environment for the 21st century:

• Visit ASCD's Whole Child Web site: www.wholechildeducation.org.

• Discuss the Whole Child Learning Compact with your colleagues. How could it affect your learning environments?

• Going beyond the four walls of the classroom may be a stretch for your school or colleagues. Discover what other teachers are doing in your school or in other schools in your area. What kinds of connections are they making technologically? What community connections are being made?

CHAPTER 5

Social Networking Through Teams

Most of your students are part of a group of friends. We used to call that a "social network." That term, however, now refers to the social networking that we do by connecting via the Internet. Susan Greenfield, a neuroscientist in Britain, warns people about the possible changes in the brain as a result of social networking, playing video games, and even watching some television programs. Her concern is about a lack of communication skills seen in some students, as well as shorter attention spans. She feels that until more studies are complete, students should be creating relationships with real people (Derbyshire, 2009).

Some of our students use social networking tools such as Twitter, blogs, wikis, texting, instant messaging, and e-mail to bond with others. With appropriate adult guidance, these interactions can be a positive experience. But our students also need face-to-face contact with peers. Those who feel socially inept on a face-to-face level may need encouragement in the classroom to join a group and interact. For these and other reasons, using flexible grouping and teams plays a critical role in educating the whole child.

Teams create endless possibilities for both the students and the teacher. Much like the one-room schoolhouse and the possibility it provided for every student to be a teacher's aide or a tutor, creating teams gives you the opportunity to surround each student with a number of peers from whom to learn. And by doing so, you may add to the self-esteem of every student in your room. We know that each child needs to feel needed. Being an integral part of a high-performance team helps meet this need. Two other needs that must be met are to be listened to and to be understood (Glenn, 1990). Teams can be a means to those ends as well.

I cannot stress enough the importance of teaming or cooperative learning in helping to develop truly healthy self-esteem. Recent brain research suggests that positive feedback provides brains with important chemicals that aid in learning and promotes self-esteem. According to Marzano, Pickering, and Pollack (2001) in *Classroom Instruction That Works*, student achievement is raised through both cooperative learning and feedback. In Chapter 4, we talked about flexible grouping—using a variety of groups for specific purposes. In this chapter, we will to address putting together teams for support. Some teachers call these "home base" teams.

Steps for Creating Power Teams

Team building is a process that, like most worthwhile endeavors, takes some time. Placing students on teams and then immediately expecting them to be able to cooperate or collaborate simply is not realistic. The steps presented here are intended to help you build highly motivated, successful *power* teams. They allow for a positive experience for both students and teachers that include a real bonding process. Groups become teams only if the individuals are equally committed, are mutually accountable, and have complementary skills. Teams can become power teams if they are also committed to personal growth and success.

We generally run into two major questions with teaming: When do I start? and How do I start? When Eric Jensen, an expert in the field of brain-compatible learning, trained me, he suggested waiting until the second week of school to begin forming teams. You may want to get to know your students if you've never taught them before. I spend one or two days setting up teams, which I do when school starts. I do this for two reasons: (1) I feel I get to know my students better as they go through the teaming process, and (2) I like to use the excitement of the first week of school to add to the team spirit. Both approaches work. You are the expert in your classroom. Choose what will work best for you.

How do you start? The steps described in the following sections have worked well for many teachers.

INSTANT MESSAGE

 You must do what is comfortable for you. If you want to start forming teams immediately and you are afraid random teams may cause discipline problems, talking to the previous year's teacher may help you avoid these problems. Another thing I do is learn my students' names before school begins by looking at the yearbook. This makes the facilitation of the teaming process easier, and I enjoy their surprise as I seem to "know" them as they begin the year.

Step 1: Form the Teams

The size of the teams will depend on the size of your class. Teams should range from a minimum of four members to a maximum of seven. You can choose the teams yourself, or you may want to draw numbers. I have taken a deck of playing cards and handed one to each student when the students enter the room. They were then divided by either suits or numbers. Other possibilities are to use birthdays, first letters of last or first names, or any other technique you like. You certainly may hand pick them or use cooperative learning groups. Here are some ways to consider grouping students if you do not use a random method:

- Learning styles—Make sure you have students from all the modalities on each team.
- Interests—Put together all the car enthusiasts, the football fans, the readers, the techies, and so on.
- Skills—Either combine students with complementary skills (one writer, one artist), or form teams composed of all writers, all artists, and so on.
- Age—Compose teams of younger students and older students.
- Heterogeneous ability—Mix students who are earning *A*s and *B*s with those earning lower grades.

- Multiple-intelligence teams—Put together students with different strengths so that each has the opportunity to offer something special to the team.
- Technology teams—In deference to the preferences of the Net Generation, I have created techno teams, in which students chose which form of technology they wanted to use to study literature. I had the Computer Literacy team, the Media Literacy team, the Digital Music team, the Smartphone Searchers, and the Information Literacy team, which used a combination of digital tools.

Step 2: Learn About Each Other

Even though many of the students may already know each other, they can benefit from getting some current information after a long summer. Discuss good listening skills with the entire class before you begin. Decide on two or three questions that you would like each team member to answer. These questions should seek information that students may not already know about their classmates. Stress to the team members that no interruptions are allowed while each member speaks. Allow 60 seconds for each student to answer a question, and realize that many students will speak for only a few seconds, especially if the group members are new to the student. You may assign a timekeeper for each team, but with younger students you may want to do the timekeeping yourself.

Here are some suggested questions:

- What's the most important thing that happened to you over the summer?
- What person in your life has influenced you more than any other?
- If you could trade places with one person in the world, who would it be?
- If you could invite three people (living or dead) over for dinner, who would you invite?
- If there was only one piece of technology equipment that you could have, what would it be and why?

Step 3: Choose Team Leaders

Team leaders can change on a weekly basis, but the first time you are forming teams, you should stress the importance of a good team leader. Tell students that the leader is a person who truly has the best interest of the team at heart. Then, explain to the class your description of the job. You may have specific duties in mind, which will depend on the age of the students you are teaching. Then simply ask the teams, "Who is willing to make a strong commitment to the team and be its leader?" Tell them that the question may be answered three ways: yes, no, or maybe. As they go around to hear the team members' responses, only someone answering with a "no" needs to give an explanation. If more than one student wants to be team leader, simply have team members decide who will lead the first week and who will lead the following weeks. When the team leaders have been decided, play some celebratory music, such as "Celebrate" or "Hallelujah," and ask them to stand up. This adds to the excitement of being a leader. At this time also model the act of applauding as a form of recognition. Explain to the teams that they may applaud at other times for their team members.

Step 4: Foster Team Spirit

This step is vital to the success of your teams. You must foster enthusiasm and make the experience as much fun as possible. Step 4 involves a few ministeps:

• Give the students 90 seconds to choose a team name. You may want to limit their choices in some ways. For instance, you may want them to choose something educational, positive, or that deals with a particular subject area. Be prepared to give a team a name if the students cannot come up with something on their own. Make your suggestion in a good-natured way, but make sure your choice is not an ideal name. You want them to try harder next time.

• Give the students three minutes to make up a cheer. This activity should be fun and easy for them. You may need to offer an example, such as "Brainiacs Are Best!"

At this point, you may be done with team spirit activities. But if you feel more are necessary, you may have them pick a team logo, mascot, or colors. You may also wish to give them a limited amount of time to make up and perform a skit.

It is important that all these activities fit the optimal learning state: *high challenge, low stress*. Adding music makes the situation less stressful, and the time constraints make these simple activities more challenging. The entire environment surrounding the teaming process should be one of fun, camaraderie, and positive spirit. If students feel stress because of the time limits, they should be reassured that you will provide more time, if needed.

Step 5: Set Individual Goals

Discuss goal setting with the class and have students offer some of their personal goals. Help them phrase their goals in a positive manner and show them how to make them specific. Have each student write three personal goals.

In our previous discussion of the reticular activating system, we learned that goals help keep this part of the brain focused on learning. Even though some of the goals that students will list may not directly relate to all of the standards or goals that you seek for their classroom learning, continually use the goal-setting strategy throughout the year for your lessons.

Here are "Seven Steps to Goal-Setting Success" that you can share with your students:

1. Tell how, what, when, and whom.
"I will babysit to earn $25 by November 15 to buy Christmas presents."
2. State your goals in the positive.
"I will behave at school," not *"I won't run in the halls."*
3. Be sure you have what you need to meet your goals.
You probably cannot learn to use a surfboard in the Midwest.
4. Ask, "Do I have control over the situation?"
You cannot control how much you will grow!
5. Make the goal the right size.
Can you earn $300 in a few weeks? Will you give up easily if the goal cannot be reached?
6. Decide how you will know when you've reached your goal.
It is easy to count money, but if your goal involves success at some endeavor, how will you know you've reached it?
7. Will your actions match your values?
Is your goal worthwhile to you? Will you feel good about achieving it?

Step 6: Set Team Goals

To measure their effectiveness, teams need to set goals that they can meet in a reasonable period of time, perhaps over the course of the grading period. Effective team goals must meet the following criteria:

1. They must be stated positively.

"We will behave in class," not *"Don't mess around in class."*

2. They must be specific.

"We will each do one extra-credit report," not *"We will do some extra credit."*

3. They must be measurable.

"Our grade point average will be 3.0," not *"We will get good grades."*

4. They must be agreed upon by the whole team. Ask students to look at their personal goals; perhaps they can combine some of those to create their team goals.

Step 7: Post the Goals

Have each team make a poster (see Figure 5.1) to display in the classroom with their team name and their goals. The posters will serve as a reminder for the teacher and will hold the students accountable. Allow the teams two to four minutes to get these written down and posted. (You may want to play some music, such as "The Sky's the Limit," while they do this.)

Figure 5.1	Sample Team Poster

Coldplay Goals

1. We will work together cooperatively.
2. We will complete all homework on time.
3. We will learn four things about the brain.
4. We will learn five different memory strategies.

Step 8: Create Team Scorecards

Have the teams create and post a chart (see Figure 5.2 on p. 64) that can be used as a scorecard. At the end of each week, they rate themselves on a scale of 1 to 10 for each category. You choose the categories, which may change each time you reorganize the teams. The chart should also have a row for "Goals Reached," which will be a percentage, rather than a score of 1 to 10. For instance, if team members have three goals and have partially completed each, they may give themselves a percentage that suggests this. Perhaps they will rate themselves at 33 percent for all three. If they have reached one goal completely, but not either of the others, they will give themselves 33 percent as well. They will have the opportunity to explain how they reached their percentage. The number of columns will depend on the number of weeks you keep your teams.

Step 9: Make Public Promises

Ask each team member to state what he or she will do for the team—for instance, "I will always be on time and do my homework." A public declaration is important. The team leader may keep track of these promises.

Figure 5.2	Team Scorecard Chart					
The Ramones						
Categories	**Weeks**					
	1	**2**	**3**	**4**	**5**	**6**
Team Spirit	8					
Cooperation	7					
Participation	9					
Contribution to the Whole	4					
Humor	8					
Homework	10					
Positive Comments	6					
Proper Grammar	5					
Average	7.1					
% Goals Reached	25					

Step 10: Make a Composite Scorecard

You may want to keep one overall scorecard (see Figure 5.3) that shows each team's name and its average score each week. An overall scorecard will make it easier to monitor the progress of the teams. This approach is effective as long as it does not stir unnecessary competition. As you can see in Figure 5.3, this chart may discourage the iTunes team. If your teams are at extremes like this, a composite card could be hurtful. However, if your teams are close in scoring, this type of chart may be motivational. You are the best judge of whether or not this will be a useful tool.

Figure 5.3	Composite Team Chart								
Teams	**Weekly Scores**								
	1	**2**	**3**	**4**	**5**	**6**	**7**	**8**	**9**
The Ramones	6.9	7.3							
Coldplay	7.2	8.0							
The iTunes	3.5	4.3							
Snarky Students	8.1	8.6							
Questioning Everything	8.6	8.7							

Creating Powerful Collaborative Relationships

We can look at the team as a tool. The team offers each member a method of expression. It also provides an avenue from which to learn, grow, and teach. What you, the teacher, must supply are the two keys to the optimal learning state: the skills to solve a problem and the knowledge that there is a solution. More specifically, keep in mind the following points as you use teaming to create powerful collaborative relationships.

1. *The main ingredient for a successful collaboration is capability.* Students must have the skills and knowledge of the subject matter to deal with the problem. They must also have some listening and thinking skills. Discuss with them the different ways in which we listen. Ask that they listen to each other, not in order to respond, but rather to be absolutely clear about what the other person is saying. Have them practice repeating the other person's message until they understand it.

2. *The team must have a challenge or a goal that everyone shares.* The goals that the team established initially may not be enough. As you assign team projects, you must create a purpose that allows the team to be a means to an end, the avenue through which the problem will be solved. Then, have the team members take that challenge or goal and get organized. What needs to be done first? Next?

3. *The team must have a safe space to do their work.* This space will be where the team members discover and discuss possibilities. It may be an area of the classroom, the library, or even a corner on the floor. The team must know that it is their space, their part of the bulletin board, or their corner of the world.

4. *The team's product should be representative of multiple intelligences, different learning styles, or varying interests in technology.* Just as teams can be formed on the basis of these criteria, it is equally important that the team product reflect that diversity. Provide appropriate assessments that take account of the skills and talents of all of the participants. You may use multiple final products to gather the many perspectives of the team members as they solve the problem.

5. *The product representations can be formed and re-formed as each member of the team appreciates the different points of view.* Give the team the opportunity and the time to play with the many ideas of its members and discover how each part adds to the whole.

6. *Allow for communication that fits the pace of the collaborators.* In other words, give the teams freedom to communicate when necessary. You may need to have a flexible schedule. Teams will work at different paces and have many different needs. Give the teams the "air space" they require.

Teaming offers a great opportunity for your digital natives to set up wikis for their projects. As noted earlier, a wiki is a Web site where all users can add and edit content, a page for organizing and coordinating information. If the teamwork involves homework and students have difficulty getting together, a wiki is an ideal "meeting place" if all team members have access to the Internet.

For instance, imagine that the iTunes team is working on a skit to show you what they know. They will need many different items for the skit. Jimmy sets up a wiki page with icons that allow it to be changed from a Web page to a working document. At the top of the page Jimmy writes "Props we will need." From a computer at home, at the library, or at another location, each team member can go to the wiki and add ideas for props. Jimmy adds another column titled "Props we have." The team members can indicate in this column which props they have access to. They can do this by simply pressing the edit button and moving the words from one column to another (see Figure 5.4). Without dozens of calls, e-mails, or text messages, the team can easily organize its project.

Figure 5.4	Sample Wiki Page
iPhone Team Skit Wiki	
EDIT	**SAVE**
Props We Need	Props We Have

7. *Allow for a change of scenery*. It is possible that a team will reach its "Aha!" moment in a unique place. If you see members of a team struggling in their space, offer them a change. A place outdoors or in the library may be where it all comes together for them.

8. *Accountability without specific jobs is key*. Many teachers have found that a problem with some cooperative learning assignments is the inflexibility on the part of the students due to assigned "jobs." Collaboration allows for a feeling of responsibility along with the knowledge that one does not have to solve the problem alone. Since the team members work as a unit, together they decide how to get the jobs

done. This way, the students can choose which job they would like to do, or they can all work together on every job.

9. *Leadership may have to make key decisions.* A team cannot always reach a unanimous decision on every move that must be made. It is expected that leaders will emerge and guide the team through a cooperative effort.

10. *Collaboration is OK.* In the team configuration, seeking help should be considered networking, not cheating. Using "experts" from other teams, other classrooms, or the world outside of school to help with the collaboration is acceptable and should be encouraged. The teams become interactive, and unless they are doing competitive projects, this approach allows students to work with others off the team as well.

11. *Having fun is part of the process.* Make team cheers part of every day. After the team finishes an assignment, remind them to do their cheer so you know they're finished. Make a video recording of their cheers. Have a Team Day, when they can dress in their team colors or wear hats. Keep the experience lively and special!

The power of teaming is exemplified by an amazing occurrence that I witnessed at a conference in New Orleans. A time crunch on one day of the presentation meant that there was only about one hour and 20 minutes to go through all the steps of the teaming process rather than the usual two-and-a-half hours. Keep in mind that this was a national conference, so participants came from all over the country. The chances of providing the proper situation to gain team spirit and rapport in a very short time were slim, but we wanted these people to have the teaming experience.

However, the system worked with time to spare. In only 45 minutes, minor miracles occurred. Teachers, administrators, and board members from Illinois, Idaho, Wisconsin, Michigan, Ohio, Florida, South Carolina, California, and Massachusetts formed some of the most cohesive, spirited, and bonded teams that I had ever seen. These people were united by following the simple steps that I have outlined for you here. A roomful of strangers became dynamic teams of people with names such as "Always Green, Always Mean" and "Blackberry Addicts." These people shared the same goals and the same dreams.

Some Final Thoughts on Teaming

During my years of sharing brain-compatible teaching and teaming, I have received countless letters and phone calls from classroom teachers. Many of their questions concern classroom management and reaching students who are having learning difficulties. A vast majority of these teachers have found that teaming helped to lessen many of their problems. Forming teams and changing your position from "knowledge keeper" to "facilitator of learning" changes the entire atmosphere of the classroom. I strongly recommend that you use this strategy. Working with others is a lifelong learning skill.

Your job as knowledge keeper is obsolete. Today's students have the ways, the means, and the speed to gather any information they want. Your new job is to guide their journey, to act as that prefrontal cortex so that they make wise decisions on where they surf the Web and what data are valid. You can lead them toward your stated goals, perhaps show them the connections they need to make, help them weed out the riff-raff, and stand back as they search, communicate, have fun, and learn!

TEXT MESSAGE

1. Before students become very involved in digital social networking, try to encourage working with students in the classroom and the school.
2. Watch your teams closely for students who seem to be loners or outsiders. It is easy to miss them when there is a lot of activity on the teams.
3. Leaders are made, not born. Give every student the opportunity to be a team leader.

CHAPTER 6

Understanding Learning Styles

------ ● ------

Learning styles have been defined in various ways by several educators. I simplify the definition by stating that your preferred learning style is *the way you receive information best*. However, we cannot stop there. Your learning style is also *the way you prefer to give feedback*, or simply your communication style. Just as you prefer either your left hand or your right hand, you prefer one modality or sense over the others. Learning styles, modalities, and senses are synonymous. Information is absorbed by the brain via one of the five senses: sight (visual), sound (auditory), touch (kinesthetic), smell (olfactory), and taste (gustatory). Smell and taste are generally lumped together under the kinesthetic category because only a small number of individuals prefer these modalities over the others. Smell and taste are also associated with movement or touch; in other words, the individual is "doing" something and therefore labeled kinesthetic.

Where does the digital world fit into learning styles? As the Net Geners and Generation Z continue to work with technology as though it were second nature, should we be looking into what this means for learning styles? Their worlds have become very visual, and this development is significant because many in the neurosciences believe that our brains are really set up more for visual information than any other kind. But technology offers something for everyone. Computer games, cell phones, blogs, and Web sites certainly provide visual information, but many provide interactive links, verbal communication, and the opportunity to move around as you please while using these learning and communication tools.

Why Understanding Learning Styles Is Important

Teaching with learning styles in mind is one of the ways we can differentiate in the classroom, so I feel it is still important to understand and use learning styles as we continue to incorporate technology into our classrooms and our lesson plans. It is believed that sometime between the ages of 4 and 7 one modality becomes established as the appropriate and comfortable way to access information from the outside world (Markova & Powell, 1998). This is not done on a conscious level, and as of this writing, it is not known whether this is a genetic circumstance or one encouraged by the environment. Whatever the case, the important thing to remember is that no learning style is better than any other. Appreciating and honoring another's learning style is a goal that could very well enhance any relationship, raise self-esteem, and contribute to quality communication. Consider the following two examples.

Case Study #1

Jamie is a very active 12-year-old girl. She plays soccer, takes dance lessons, and is on the student council at her middle school. Jamie's preferred modality is visual. She enjoys reading, understands maps easily (she usually is the navigator on family trips), and often says, "Picture this . . ."

Because of her busy schedule, her room is one that her mother once described as a "disaster." Clothes were often on the floor, and her mom couldn't tell if they were clean or dirty. It seemed as though every morning on the way out the door, her mom would yell, "Jamie, clean your room when you get home from practice!" Yet every day the room remained the same or became messier.

Upon reading about learning styles, Jamie's mother decided to try a new approach. She began to leave Jamie notes around the house. She began with a note on Jamie's bedroom door. It read, "Jamie, please clean your room by doing the following . . ." That first list was a long one, but to her mother's surprise and pleasure, Jamie cleaned her room that day.

Understanding a learning style and then communicating to that style can make enormous differences in parent-child relationships. Jamie cooperated, and the mother-daughter relationship improved as her mom did less yelling and Jamie completed her tasks.

Case Study #2

Jeremy was having a difficult time learning his multiplication tables. The teacher sent home several notes asking his parents to work with him and stressing the importance of the task. When confronted by his parents, Jeremy complained that the numbers got all fuzzy on the page and he couldn't remember them. As his parents tried to work with him at the dining room table, Jeremy fidgeted and played with the napkin holder and then the salt shaker, and finally managed to kick his dad under the table. His dad became furious, threw the book down, and gave up.

As you may have guessed, Jeremy is a kinesthetic learner. For his brain to function, Jeremy needs movement or touch. At home it may be helpful for him to simply walk around the dining room table as he repeats the multiplication tables after his parents. Another fun way for Jeremy to learn might be to put the multiplication tables to music or a beat. If he could recite a problem and an answer with a rhythmic chant, that movement might be enough to keep him on task.

The important first step in understanding and dealing with different learning styles is to become a keen observer and recognize the differences in the ways people take in information and communicate. To do this, we begin with descriptions of the three basic modalities.

Visual Learners: Seeing Is Believing

The visual learner can usually sit still for long periods of time. This individual writes well, and usually spells and proofreads well. A visual learner likes lists as a way to keep organized. Visual order is not only appreciated, but may also be necessary for clear thinking.

Visual learners often speak rapidly. If he or she is right-handed, this learner will usually look up and to the left to retrieve information. This information is in picture form, and as the individual is putting words to the pictures, there is a tendency for rapid speech. The speed at which the pictures are seen can account for incomplete sentences and "ums" and "likes."

Visual learners have specific words that they often use in their speech. These words are indicative of their visual preference. For instance, visual learners may say

- "I get the picture."
- "Show me."
- "Looks good to me."
- "This isn't very clear."

Visual learners may connect most easily with you and others through eye contact. When these learners are upset or angry, they may roll their eyes. They will be easily distracted by movement and tend to watch and follow any movement in a room.

Visual learners may be either print adapted or environment adapted. They are sometimes a little of both. Print-adapted visual learners are adept at learning every-thing they read. Environment-adapted visual learners remember their surroundings and notice details. An environment-adapted visual learner will notice what you are wearing and whether your hair is in place. Spots on the carpet may not go unnoticed by these learners.

To help your visual learners, you can do the following:

- Limit visual distractions while these learners are working.
- Recognize that looking at material is the ideal way for these individuals to learn, so while you are explaining an idea or a concept, draw pictures or use visual representations.
- Show your visual learners how to do something before expecting them to do it alone.
- Use lists and notes.
- Take advantage of the fact that maps, graphs, pictures, worksheets, and even information in the textbook are valuable resources for these learners.
- Watch facial expressions to check for frustration, confusion, or apathy.

Auditory Learners: Sounds Good to Me

Auditory learners tend to talk a lot. They may even talk to themselves. Do not be alarmed at this behavior; it is natural and normal for an auditory learner. However, the distraction in the classroom can be very annoying to teachers and other students. Once a student realizes a preference for auditory learning, that information can be used to adapt to situations rather than excuse them. These learners talk easily to others and are comfortable interacting in this way. Auditory learners usually have extensive vocabularies and use their voices purposefully when they speak—that is, there are usually changes in tonality and rhythm when they speak. This makes listening to them interesting.

Auditory learners speak more slowly than visual learners. Imagine that they are listening to a tape recorder in their heads where they have stored the information they are sharing. The tape plays slowly so the learner has the opportunity to articulate. This is a very comfortable situation for the auditory learner as long as questions aren't asked in a haphazard fashion, which causes the tape to be fast-forwarded or rewound as the information is sought. It can be a slow and frustrating experience for the auditory learner.

Auditory learners also have specific words that they use in their speech. It may be easy to identify them if you listen carefully. They may say

- "That's music to my ears."
- "I hear you."
- "That's clear as a bell."
- "Sounds like a plan."

Auditory learners connect well through discussion. They may interrupt others often and need to be aware of this potential problem. Some auditory learners have difficulty reading because confronting a lot of visual stimulation may cause them to space out.

To help auditory learners, you can do the following:

- Avoid unnecessary sounds that may be distracting.
- Encourage discussion and seeking the learners' opinions.
- Read aloud to these students or have them read aloud to you.
- Have recorded books available.

• Use teamwork and cooperative learning to provide additional opportunities for these students to speak.

Kinesthetic Learners: Let's Get Physical

Kinesthetic learners vary. One type wiggles and jiggles until someone goes crazy, and the other wants to be in a very comfortable position and looks ready for sleep. Both types require movement or touch to learn. Kinesthetic learners need to attach strong emotions to what they are learning. These individuals are the most difficult to deal with in a traditional classroom simply because they are not traditional learners.

Some learners with a kinesthetic preference speak very slowly because they are waiting to attach feelings to what they say. You may find you have a tendency to want to finish sentences for these learners. These students may be distracted by temperature changes and other alterations in comfort levels.

Kinesthetic learners may reveal something about their modality preference by using specific words and phrases. Listen carefully to them and you may hear them say

- "I don't get it."
- "Get a grip on yourself."
- "Give me a concrete example."
- "I can't get a handle on that."

Kinesthetic learners require movement or touch to activate their brains. The least stressful way to approach them is as though they are blind and deaf. Kinesthetic learners may be unaware of the sound of your voice or even a waving motion. Until these learners are touched or until they move, their other senses are literally not awakened.

To help your kinesthetic learners, you can do the following:

- Use as many hands-on activities as possible for learning.
- Provide opportunities for movement.
- Walk with them while discussing information.
- Touch their hands or shoulders to get their attention.
- Provide comfortable surroundings for learning activities.

Modality Messages

Perhaps you are beginning to associate the described characteristics with either yourself or others you know. You may be saying to yourself, "So that's why I do that!" Once you understand your own preferred modality and those of others, positive changes can occur in your relationships. So Jamie, in the first case study related earlier, might say, "So Mom really doesn't hate me! She's auditory and I'm visual; she's always yelling about how messy my room is, but I really don't even notice the mess!" Understanding and honoring others' preferred modality is, in essence, "speaking their language." It enables you to enter other people's worlds, which can enhance rapport.

Over the years I have realized that learning takes no time at all—it's *not* learning that takes all the time! If, to quote from the movie *Cool Hand Luke*, "what we have here is a failure to communicate," learning is difficult. But once information is presented in the proper modality, learning can be easier and more fun.

Perhaps you know someone who had the experience of being in a classroom where nothing seemed to sink in, but his or her sibling had the same teacher and learned a great deal. What probably occurred was not a personality conflict, but rather a learning style conflict.

Your communication modality is what makes "sense" to you. It's the easiest way to take in information and the most natural way to give it back. Some students and adults love to give oral presentations. They much prefer that option over written reports or projects. Those of you who are not auditory may break out in a cold sweat at the mere thought of getting up in front of others to speak. You would prefer writing a 50-page paper or creating an extensive project *as long as you don't have to speak*!

We have all become comfortable with our communication style. Some of us hate to talk on the phone. Many of us would rather watch athletic events than participate. Others don't understand why we're reading when we could be out *doing* something! It is our style that makes us who we are and makes the world a more interesting place.

The purpose in understanding all of this is to make learning, both academic and social, easier and more meaningful. To be able to connect with our worlds in a positive way and feel good about ourselves is a much sought after goal. If we, as parents and teachers, can help the next generation accomplish their goals and fulfill their dreams, then we will have served our purposes as models and educators.

At the same time, our communication is only as good as the response that we get. In other words, when the response that we get from another is not the response that we expected, it is time to examine what and how we communicated. An example would be asking a kinesthetic learner to take out the garbage while she is watching television. Probably nothing will happen. Remember what I suggested earlier about thinking of kinesthetic learners as being blind and deaf? Touching the kinesthetic learner on the shoulder, getting her attention, and then making the same request could result in some action. Similarly, reciting a grocery list out loud to a visual learner may result in missing items, whereas a written list would make you both happy. (You'd get the groceries and the visual learner would have the list to refer to.) On the other hand, giving an auditory learner a list may be an insult, and he won't read it anyway!

To help you speak the same language as others in your life, here are lists of suggested messages for each modality:

• Visual messages: an eyeful; appears to me; bird's-eye view; clear cut; dim view; eye to eye; hazy idea; in view of; looks like; make a scene; mental picture; mind's eye; naked eye; paint a picture; plainly see; pretty as a picture; see to it; sight for sore eyes; staring into space; take a peek; tunnel vision

• Auditory messages: blabber mouth; clear as a bell; clearly expressed; call on; give you an earful; express yourself; give me your ear; grant an audience; hear what I'm saying; hold your tongue; idle talk; loud and clear; manner of speaking; purrs like a kitten; rings a bell; tattle-tale; to tell the truth; tongue-tied; unheard of; well informed; within hearing range; word for word

• Kinesthetic messages: chip off the old block; come to grips with; control yourself; cool, calm, and collected; firm foundation; get a handle on; get in touch with; get the drift; hand in hand; hang in there; hold it; hold on; keep your shirt on; light-headed; pull some strings; smooth operator; start from scratch; stiff upper lip; stuffed shirt; too much of a hassle; topsy-turvy; underhanded

INSTANT MESSAGE

Computer use can be a visual-auditory-kinesthetic activity when students work together. They are looking at programs or Web sites, they talk about the topic, and they are allowed to use the mouse, press keys, and move around.

How High Is Your "Eye Cue"?

In addition to the various indicators described previously, another way to determine the communication style of any individual is by watching eye movements. Our eyes indicate which sense we are using to access information (see Figure 6.1). This information can be very helpful in simple skills like spelling. The best way to learn to spell is visually. If you can visualize the word, you have a much better chance of spelling it correctly. If a student is not looking up to "see" the word, watch where his eyes go. If the eyes are looking to the side, indicating an auditory learner trying to sound out the word, check to see if the word can be spelled phonetically. If it cannot, suggest to the student that he look up and to the left (if he is right-handed). Auditory learners do have visual capabilities and this may help. For the kinesthetic learner who looks down, you must tell him to look up. Unless he has extremely strong feelings about the word, all he will find by looking down is that he feels dumb not knowing the word. To put it simply,

- Visual learners look up.
- Auditory learners look to the side.
- Kinesthetic learners look down.

Watching eye movements alone does not provide enough evidence to determine a communication style. However, this information along with asking questions and paying attention to phrases linked to modalities can lead to an accurate determination. Ruby Payne (1998) finds eye accessing cues helpful when working with students from poverty.

If you have a hunch about a person's style, continue your investigation by asking a few questions. These need not be personal questions, and this experience can be fun and enlightening. Simply ask certain questions and observe where the eyes go as the person searches for answers.

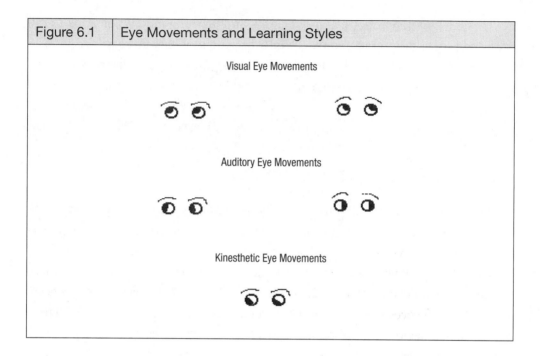

Figure 6.1 | Eye Movements and Learning Styles

Visual Eye Movements

Auditory Eye Movements

Kinesthetic Eye Movements

For visual learners, ask questions such as these: *What color are your mother's eyes? When was the last time you saw* _____ *on television?* These are questions that cause visual learners to recall information that is already known. They will look up briefly to the right or the left. Other questions require a creative response: *Can you imagine a purple dog with yellow stripes?* In this case, visual learners will look up in the opposite direction from the direction they used for visual recall.

For the auditory learner, ask questions such as these: *When was the last time you heard "America, the Beautiful"? Do you remember what I said to you this morning?* The auditory learner will look to the side to access information from the "audiocassette player" in the brain. Like the visual learner, the auditory learner accesses one side for recalling information and the other side for creating information. If you ask, *What would your father say if you didn't come home on time?* the response would be a creative one, and the auditory learner would look to the opposite side to create the information.

For the kinesthetic learner, you might ask questions such as these: *How are you feeling right now?* or *What does it feel like to get caught with your hand in the cookie jar?* To catch the rapid eye movements, one usually needs more than one question.

This information about eye movements and learning modalities adds to our knowledge of how we communicate. Our eyes send modality messages.

When students are asked a question and don't know the answer, they may feel bad and look down even though their preferred learning style is visual or auditory. You can ask them to look up for the information if you believe they are visual learners and to the side if you believe they are auditory learners.

Learning Styles and Technology

Remember that learning style is generally the same as communication style. We all take information in through one of our senses and we communicate to others through that same sense. We can discover another's communication style by listening to their verbal messages, observing their eye movements, listening to the speed of their speech, observing how they "teach" others, and observing their actions. Understanding and speaking to another's communication style is a way to "speak the same language" and gain rapport. In addition, our self-esteem is raised when someone speaks or teaches to our communication style.

In our efforts to offer digital choices to our students, we can categorize and match some of those choices according to learning style. For the visual learner, videos, Web sites, text messaging, and movies on an iPod may be interesting. The auditory learner may like group work around the computer, music on an iPod, and audio conferencing via the Internet. Kinesthetic learners may be attracted to Internet searches, using an iPod or iPhone, and anything with buttons to push or things to touch.

TEXT MESSAGE

The digital world is full of visual information, and the brain is set up to process more visual information than any other kind. Honor each learner's strength, but encourage students to "stretch" and use the visual modality more. Students who are comfortable with high-tech devices and curious about the cyberworld will extend their learning styles to keep up, catch up, and get ahead.

CHAPTER 7

The Digital Native and Intelligence

—————— 🌐 ——————

A new student came into my classroom right after Christmas. He'd been kicked out of two schools for what were called "behavior problems." I spent the first few days just observing him and waiting for some bizarre behavior. Nothing happened. He didn't catch on to much. His homework was rarely done, and he had some interesting excuses. After several weeks of waiting for his previous grades to be sent from the last school, I called. He had received mostly *D*s and *F*s.

He seemed like a good kid. When I called on him, he usually had an answer. His oral reading skills were certainly acceptable for a 7th grader. But he never smiled. When we formed new teams, he seemed totally apathetic about the entire experience.

We covered a mythology unit. The whole class was receptive to the myths I shared with them. Even he seemed mildly interested. We put together booklets with lots of pictures of gods and goddesses to color. Everyone was pretty excited about it. (Many people don't realize how much students, no matter what age, like to color.) He did his booklet with no more enthusiasm than anything else he had done for me.

I was really ready to write him off as one of those kids who have too many problems at home for me to help. I decided that he spent too much time in a state of fear to acquire any knowledge from me.

In English class we began the chapter that covers prepositions, conjunctions, and interjections. I always begin this unit with music. I use special music consisting of songs that previous years' students have made up in order to learn 60 prepositions.

I assigned each team an equal number of prepositions. They were then given instructions that they had to make up a song using these words. They had the option to use a familiar tune, which I assured them was very helpful in this situation, or they could make up their own. I gave them about 30 minutes for this project.

By the end of the period, they were ready to sing. The new student's team was third on the schedule. Because of band practice, only two people were present that day on his team. The other team member was very embarrassed and had trouble participating, so the new student sang their song by himself. He stayed on key. He knew the words. And he smiled . . . for the first time, he smiled.

We applauded for each team. When we applauded him, he beamed. I told him what a great job he had done, and I mentioned that I needed to use music more often. He smiled again and nodded.

This is not an unusual story. We've all experienced similar situations. We can sit back and remember those moments when we got "lucky" and found the key to unlock a child's mind. We can be proud of the fact that we don't give up easily. But we can't rely on luck anymore. Too much information is available for us to use to help our students. Some of that information is written in books with recipes for us to follow, but teachers know that not all students will follow that recipe. Educators who use differentiated instruction are offering students many choices as well. The student I described in the anecdote is a member of Generation X; a Net Gen student's story could be quite different.

The Net Gens would probably download their music from their iPod or MP3 player. The students would pass around the music player with earphones so each team member could listen. Discussion would follow. In my classroom, that discussion would be verbal. In some high-tech classrooms the conversation would be conducted with text messaging on their phones or instant messaging on their computers. A student with considerable technology skills might digitally enhance the music using his own equipment, change the melody, and even add the words so all members could now hear the song with the assigned words.

Students don't just use technology passively. They interact with it. As Tapscott (2009) points out, students can now change the content on certain Web sites they search. Think of how it would have been for you as a student. Did you ever have the opportunity to correct errors in your history book? Could you add newer content to your science book?

This is the generation we are teaching. They are bright and talented, and their mission in school and in life is different from that of previous generations.

Multiple Intelligences: What Are They?

Howard Gardner was co-director of Project Zero at Harvard University in 1972. The project was part of the Graduate School of Education and its purpose was to find ways to enhance learning and cognition. Through this work, Gardner created the theory of Multiple Intelligences, which explored the idea that there is more than one way of being smart. In 1983, he published *Frames of Mind*, which outlines his theory of seven intelligences. He later added an eighth and a ninth intelligence. For educational purposes, we will focus on the first eight intelligences (Gardner, 1983).

1. **Bodily-Kinesthetic**—These students want to move around a lot, and they use their bodies to get things done.

2. **Interpersonal**—These students love to talk and may be excellent leaders because of their ability to solve problems.

3. **Intrapersonal**—These students like reading and solitude and are good at understanding others' experiences.

4. **Logical-Mathematical**—These students have excellent problem-solving and math skills.

5. **Musical-Rhythmic**—These students may hum and tap in class; they may not be singers, but they have the ability to use sounds and rhythm.

6. **Spatial**—These students are good at understanding the relationships between things. Spatial students often like to design and draw.

7. **Verbal-Linguistic**—These students like to talk. They often argue, debate, or tell stories.

8. **Naturalist**—These students are interested in nature. Classifying animals, insects, or leaves may be compelling activities for them.

Each of these intelligences is valuable to have on a team. A multiple-intelligence team can be composed of one person from each area. The team may experience less conflict when each member has his or her own area of expertise. I have found this team configuration to work well.

Multiple Intelligence Assessment

Although multiple-intelligence tests are available, I prefer to allow individuals to assess themselves. Many questions on formal assessments can be perceived in different ways, and some learners have difficulty with standardized paper-and-pencil assessments. So I simply explain the intelligences to my students and let them decide where their strengths lie. They can list the intelligences on paper and use a scale of 1 to 10, with 10 indicating they are almost expert in the area, and 1 indicating they need a lot of work in that area and it may be uncomfortable for them.

Our educational system values verbal-linguistic and mathematical-logical intelligences more than others. But, in fact, we each possess all eight of the intelligences; some are simply more fully developed than others. The key is to teach to all of these intelligences. The methods are relatively simple.

Beginning at the start of school, it may take you up to four weeks to identify your students' intelligence preferences. You can try some of the written assessments available online. If you don't feel they are appropriate, you can undertake purposeful observation instead. That, along with a self-assessment by the students, should provide what you need to determine your students' intelligences.

What should you look for? Here are some indicators:

- Verbal-Linguistic
  - Thinks and speaks precisely
  - Chatters constantly
  - Remembers details

- Logical-Mathematical
  - Uses logical reasoning
  - Solves problems quickly
  - Has good math skills
- Visual-Spatial
  - Enjoys puzzles, pictures, drawing
  - Needs pictures for understanding
- Bodily-Kinesthetic
  - Likes hands-on assignments
  - Has difficulty sitting still
  - Is good at sports
- Musical-Rhythmic
  - Hums while working or walking
  - Taps out a beat on the desk
- Interpersonal
  - Shares easily
  - Is a good listener
  - Is a good leader
- Intrapersonal
  - Is quiet, reflective
  - Enjoys being alone
  - Likes to read
- Naturalist
  - Likes to be outdoors
  - Observes plants, animals
  - Notices relationships in nature

In an ideal situation we would teach to all the intelligences and simultaneously develop each of these intelligences in each student. In many cases, this ideal is asking for more than we have time to accomplish. Being more pragmatic, I believe an alternative is to involve students in projects that integrate the intelligences. If your school supports team teaching, plan some projects with other teachers and carry out these plans to integrate the intelligences. In so doing, you will serve your students and their intelligences very well. Teaching and learning that cover all eight intelligences may give students the opportunity to master material that they have never been able to handle before. The opportunities are endless for allowing students to learn in their preferred ways. The next section describes one of my own experiences.

INSTANT MESSAGE

 In the real world our students will be in career situations that will require them to integrate these ways of learning, as well as various subject areas. Integrated projects offer an opportunity for them to understand how the different intelligences and areas are related and are useful in their lives.

A Multiple Intelligence Project

I had always helped with the school plays. One year we wanted to do something other than the Shakespeare and Dickens productions from previous years, and I convinced my colleagues to have the students write their own play. This was a perfect opportunity to use the multiple intelligences. Some simple preplanning with the other teachers helped us include many subject areas. The content of the story was based on information learned in a unit on eating disorders that was taught by the science teacher. The topic had also come up in a discussion of the media and critical thinking and reading.

The students wrote a play called "The Brady Bunch Goes Bananas," and here is how the intelligences became incorporated in the project:

- Verbal-Linguistic—These students chose to write the script.
- Logical-Mathematical—These students helped by predicting outcomes and casting parts.
- Visual-Spatial—These students designed the scenery and set the stage.
- Bodily-Kinesthetic—These students were the stars of the show. They acted and danced, and some students changed the scenery.
- Musical-Rhythmic—These students chose the music and sound effects and were in charge of timing for sounds and lines.

- Interpersonal—These students directed, organized, and were in charge of conflict resolution.
- Intrapersonal—These students assigned character emotions and observed the effects of characters on each other.
- Naturalist—These students added to the stage set by bringing in plants and encouraging the addition of natural events to the play.

Of course, many of the students had more than one job to fill in the production of the play. They chose what they wanted to do, and they chose what was comfortable for them. We discussed the intelligences with them and let them decide which areas they would excel in. The teachers made the students comfortable by first sharing their own self-assessments on the multiple intelligences. The students then had the opportunity to assess themselves.

Multiple Intelligence Projects in the Digital Age

Today's students would approach the play production in a much different way. The main characters might find clips on YouTube of the Bradys and use some of their actual plot ideas, mannerisms, and corny jokes. Along with the actors, the scenery people could explore several Brady Bunch Web sites to see pictures of the house, the backyard, and the bedrooms, and then create something more modern but with a "Brady" flair. Those in charge of music could download music used on the show, change some of it, and hook it up to speakers. Interpersonal students might text information to the actors to offer suggestions for changes without saying a word out loud. This could prevent embarrassment to the performers as well as mediate any conflict. Of course, the play would be video recorded and uploaded to your school Web site.

If you are concerned that use of digital media might get out of control, be sure to set rules and consequences for those who break them. A high-tech environment for learning has no room for text messages that criticize or make fun of another student, for example.

Teaching with and to the intelligences is an experience that will awaken the intelligences of some of the students you may have been ready to give up on. We know above all else that we are in this profession to do whatever it takes to give students the opportunity to learn. Using these methods will provide you with some opportunities to grow as well.

TEXT MESSAGE

Look at your own areas of expertise. Those areas in which you are able to consistently go beyond what many of your colleagues can accomplish, where mistakes rarely occur, and where you require little effort are the intelligence areas that you prefer. Are they more than the usual verbal-linguistic or mathematical-logical intelligences? If they are, can you share these in some way with your students? By trying to enhance your own areas of intelligence, you will automatically add to your students' growth and experiences.

PART 3

Music, Mind Maps, and Memory

In a brain-compatible classroom there are always choices. The brain loves music, and the digital brain will respond to various approaches to using it. Because vision is the dominant sense for most of us, creating visuals such as mind maps will help many of our students. Understanding how memory works leads to a wide variety of strategies to motivate students and move information into long-term memory.

CHAPTER 8

The Digital Brain and Music

1971: For my first teaching job, I bring in the stereo I had in college. It has a turntable and two detachable speakers. It plays records. I use it to add music to some of the units I am teaching.

1982: I am teaching high school students. I bring in a boom box. It plays and records audiocassettes. I add music to some of the units I am teaching.

1989: I am teaching in a K–8 building. I bring in my new boom box. It plays audio-cassettes and has a CD player as well. I play only cassettes because CDs are too expensive and too easily damaged. I add music to some of the units I am teaching, and I use melodies to sing information as a way to help my students' memories.

1994: I am teaching in an affluent middle school. I proudly plug in my flashy new, improved, small, round, red boom box. It plays audiocassettes and has a CD player with a remote control. I use music for classroom management, as a memory aid, and to control stress in the classroom. I play cassettes and CDs. I make copies of my purchased CDs and use the copies at school so if they are damaged it doesn't cost too much to replace them.

2009: I give keynote addresses, speak at conferences, and do professional development at schools all over the country. I bring my iPod with me everywhere. It contains all of the music I will need and it weighs less than an ounce. I also bring iPod speakers that are quite small but can project sound throughout a room. I don't have to worry about students scratching a CD, but I do worry occasionally about someone stealing this nifty music maker.

Today's students walk through the halls at school plugged in to their MP3 players or their cell phones. They have an iTunes account and download music constantly. Not using music for today's techno student is brain antagonistic!

Even before the current prevalence of music playing devices, we've known that one of the most powerful techniques ever developed for learners has been the use of music in the classroom. Many studies suggest that people are affected by different types of music. Music carries its own signals that can affect the emotional center of the brain and also enhance long-term memory (Webb & Webb, 1990). Through my years of training, practicing, and working with teachers all over the United States, I am convinced that using music in the classroom benefits learning, self-esteem, and rapport. The process of using music is not complicated. With practice and patience you can be a master of music.

Current Research on Music

Most of the research on music is based on playing musical instruments. Here are some recent findings:

• A study by researchers at Northwestern University provides evidence that playing a musical instrument significantly enhances the brain stem's sensitivity to speech sounds (Wong et al., 2007).

• Music lessons taken in school or out of school are positively associated with academic achievement in reading and math (Wiley-Blackwell, 2009).

• Children exposed to music lessons for three years showed improvement in two specific reading subskills—vocabulary and verbal sequencing (SAGE Publications, 2009).

• Young children who take music lessons show improvement in memory over the course of one year (Oxford University Press, 2006).

There are many reasons why music education should be encouraged in school. Unfortunately, it is often one of the first areas that is cut when funding for schools becomes an issue. Providing music in the classroom may help build an appreciation of different kinds of music among your students and encourage some of them to take lessons that may improve their confidence, organizational skills, and cognitive ability.

Mood Music

To truly comprehend the benefits of music, we must understand that there are four distinct brain "states" that correspond to four kinds of brain waves: beta, alpha, theta, and delta. These states reflect the electrical activity of the brain and the number of cycles per second in the brain waves being produced:

• *The beta wave*, cycling at 12 to 40 cycles per second, is the brain wave of the conscious mind. It is in this state that we accomplish our everyday activities. This is our "run-see-go-do" state. In this state we are wide awake and able to problem solve.

• *The alpha wave*, cycling at 8 to 12 cycles per second, is the brain wave that signifies relaxed alertness. It is in this state that memory is enhanced and facts are more easily absorbed.

• *The theta wave*, cycling at 4 to 7 times per second, is the brain wave that occurs just as we drift off to sleep and as we awaken. It indicates a deep meditative state of high suggestibility and great creativity.

• *The delta wave*, cycling at 1 to 3 cycles per second, is the brain wave that occurs as we sleep. Learning does not take place in this state.

The alpha state is the preferred learning state and can be accessed on a conscious level. Although the theta state is a highly receptive state, it cannot be easily accessed. Be aware that in our waking states several different types of waves are present in our brains. For example, we actually have some alpha waves and a few theta waves present during our beta time. What we are looking for in the classroom is a way to access the best possible state for learning. Thus, the alpha state can be accessed through certain kinds of music.

Between 1600 and 1750, music was composed according to a mathematical formula. Because of its unique harmony and sound, this music, called baroque music, could balance the body and mind by regulating heart rate, respiration, and brain waves. Most of the pieces composed during this period averaged 45 to 60 beats per minute and brought about a state of relaxation for the listener.

Playing baroque music during a testing period has been shown to increase test scores by an average of 10 percent. For most students, this kind of music is relaxing and reduces test anxiety. Furthermore, it induces the alpha state for the brain, which allows for memory enhancement (Rose & Nicholl, 1997).

Baroque music aids in the whole-brain approach to learning. Although brain activity occurs in both hemispheres, many individuals have *more* activity on one side. When a conversation is in progress, most of the activity takes place in the left hemisphere. If music is added to the conversation, the right hemisphere becomes more active. We know that music can aid in whole-brain learning in this way. If music is added to the conversation, the right hemisphere becomes more active. Learning is a whole-brain process. By activating both the left and the right hemispheres, we enhance learning and provide more connections to the material.

Music by the following baroque composers would be appropriate for classroom use during testing and other quiet times:

- Arcangelo Corelli (1653–1713)
- Antonio Vivaldi (1678–1741)
- Johann Sebastian Bach (1685–1750)
- George Frideric Handel (1685–1759)

The period of music following the baroque period was the classical period, from 1750 to 1825. Classical music differs from baroque in several respects, the most important being the number of beats per minute, which is usually 60 to 80. This music is not as relaxing as baroque music. However, classical music has its place in the classroom.

Classical music will inspire the brain. It is useful for problem solving and creativity (Malyarenko et al., 1996). As groups or teams work on projects, classical music would be appropriate to play in the background. It can also be used as background music during storytelling. Here are some composers of classical music to choose from:

- Franz Josef Haydn (1732–1809)
- Wolfgang Amadeus Mozart (1756–1791)
- Ludwig van Beethoven (1770–1827)

Memory Music

It is important to note here that music can be more than background sound. The full effect of music on memory is becoming clearer as researchers continue to study the brain. Whether you believe in the left/right brain theory, which states that brain activity related to music is located in the right hemisphere, where the emotions are also located, or if you believe in the triune brain theory, which states that emotions and music are both located in the limbic system, the fact is that attaching information to emotion enhances memory and recall. The memory structure, the hippocampus, is located in the limbic system. It makes sense to use music as a way to store information in long-term memory because both music and memory are located in the same area of the brain. Think about this: how did each of us learn the alphabet? That alphabet song has stayed with us forever. From where did that tune come? Do you remember "Twinkle, Twinkle, Little Star?"

The mind enjoys rhythm and rhyme. Taking new vocabulary and putting it to a familiar tune will help your students learn and remember. Better yet, have them choose the tune and put the vocabulary words to music themselves. Many publishers are now linking information with music. Check with the publisher of your texts to see if any related music is available.

Management Music

The use of music—both turning it on and turning it *off*—can be a signal to your students that they should prepare for what happens next. Letting the music manage your class is fun, enjoyable for the students, and quite easy. Here are some simple suggestions:

- Have a special song playing as the students enter the room. When it is time for class to begin, simply turn off the music. The students will soon realize that when the music ends, it's time to get serious.

- Play a certain song for breaks. Time it so you and the students know that they have a certain number of minutes to get their drinks of water or attend to other needs. Let them know that they must be back in their seats when the song ends. They will soon have the break down to a science, and you won't have stragglers.

- When you need your class to do something quickly, play some fast-paced music. For instance, if you decide to change the arrangement of the students' desks, describe the new arrangement and tell them when the music starts to begin quietly moving their desks to the new spot. Start the music and see how quickly the job gets done. If you want to do some action research, try the activity with a different group of students without using music. I bet the task will take longer and the students will be noisier.

- Play a specific song at the end of the day to signify that it's time to clean up and get ready to go home. The students must have their desks in order and their book bags packed before the song ends. This is an enjoyable way to end the day.

These four simple suggestions can make a big difference in how organized your class and your day become. As you become accustomed to using music, you will develop your own ideas for using it for the express purpose of classroom management.

Music for Discussion

At a recent conference I wanted to say hello to a colleague who was presenting across the hall from me. I always start playing music before I set up the rest of my equipment. As the participants entered and sat down, most began talking to one another. When I finished with my setup, I walked quietly out of the room and dashed across the hall to say hello.

As I entered my friend's presentation room, I started to say hello from the back of the room. I stopped when I realized how quiet his room was. The participants were sitting down and no one was talking! As a result, I walked up to my friend and whispered my hello. We chatted quietly for a few moments and then I hurried back to my room, where the chatter was a little louder than before due to the entrance of some more participants.

Why was there such a difference in conversation between the two rooms? The background music is the answer. When music is playing, people are more inclined to speak because they don't think outsiders will be listening to their conversation.

When you play some background music as your students work together in small groups, the same phenomenon will occur. Give it a try, and I am sure you will see a difference in the quality and quantity of conversation.

Music with a Purpose: Where Do You Begin?

You may want to start using music slowly, unless this is something you are very comfortable with. I used to tell teachers that if they weren't comfortable, they shouldn't use music at all. I have now "changed my tune"! Using music provides too many benefits, and there are opportunities with music that should not be missed. Give it a try.

In terms of equipment, it doesn't matter which device you use—tape player, CD player, or iPod—as long as it works for you. Your students will be more impressed with an MP3 player or an iPod, and if these devices are new to you, you can let them "teach" you about the ways of the techno-music world.

You will find that after you get started, your students will provide some of the music. In the meantime, check the library for tapes and CDs that you can preview. Inexpensive music is available at discount stores and online. Your school's kindergarten teacher is probably an excellent source of fun songs for special occasions like birthdays and for movement activities.

Here are some additional ideas for using music with various purposes in mind, along with suggestions for specific pieces that might be suitable.

• *Opening class*—As I suggested in the section on music for classroom management, play a specific tune or tunes every day as the students enter the room. The music will contribute to the sense of ritual, and as you'll recall from Chapter 3, rituals help provide students with a sense of security. The music can also elicit a state of readiness.

Example: "Whistle While You Work"

- *Closing class*—Playing a special song can signal it's time to clean up, pack up, and wait for further instructions.

Example: "Happy Trails to You"

- *Celebrations*—Use different songs when you return papers or tests. Have music ready if the school wins a basketball game or a speech tournament. Birthday songs are great, even for older students.

Example: "1812 Overture"

- *Introducing new material*—Music used for this purpose should be slow and played quietly in the background. Only instrumental music will do for this category.

Example: Slow movements from Vivaldi's "Four Seasons"

- *Problem solving*—Classical music works well here, and some New Age tunes would work as well.

Example: Beethoven's "Ode to Joy"

- *Relaxation*—Baroque music slows things down. Some selections from hit movies will also do the trick.

Example: Theme from "Beauty and the Beast"

- *Test time*—Baroque music is the only choice for this purpose. Some modern composers sell music that has 60 beats per minute, and they recommend playing their music during testing. Unless they can give you research suggesting that their music raises test scores, be cautious.

Example: Handel's "Water Music"

- *Storytelling*—Classical music is best for this activity. You want some energy.

Example: "Dance of the Sugar Plum Fairy"

- *Brainstorming*—Choose music that gets the ideas flowing and the emotions involved.

Example: Theme from "Chariots of Fire"

- *Stretching*—Stretching is a great way to change states. You may want two types of music: one for slower stretching and one for fast.

Examples: Fats Domino's "I'm Walking" and selections from "Hooked on Classics"

INSTANT MESSAGE

If you have colleagues using music in the classroom, discuss which pieces you are using, especially for classroom management. A 1st grade teacher in one school used the same song for clean-up time that one of her colleagues used as background music. When the background music was started, students immediately stopped working and began to clean up!

Some Final Thoughts

If you do nothing else in your classroom with music, play Baroque music during test taking. A few students may object at first, but ask them to give it five minutes and see if they adjust. You may also try moving them as far from the music as possible. If they do not adjust, see if you can place them in another room for the test or if they can take it later. As mentioned earlier, playing baroque music during a test is known to raise test scores 10 percent. It is worth trying for the sake of your students. You might also want to play music during study time and rest time. It may make a big difference in the climate of your room.

One word of caution is necessary. Some of your students may have negative associations with certain music—that is, they associate certain songs or tunes with specific times in their lives. These pieces of music may elicit an undesirable state of mind that is not conducive to learning. It is impossible to avoid this situation entirely. Using music from eras your students may not be familiar with will lessen the potential for negative effects. For this reason, I prefer old show tunes or music from the '50s and '60s. Again, use music that makes you comfortable, and just be aware of the possibilities.

Educate your students about the music. Let them know that you are introducing music into the classroom to help them. Tell them the music will improve their memories and their grades. To demonstrate this effect, have them memorize a list of items for you by putting them to a familiar tune. Remind them that they learned the alphabet by first learning a song. This information should help convince them that this is a worthwhile endeavor. Besides, they will probably all love the music.

When you make the commitment to use music, stick to it. When I first began, I chose Disney favorites for my morning music. My homeroom students were 8th graders. The first day they entered the room and heard the music, they laughed at me. They said the music was "stupid" and told me to turn it off. I thought about changing the music or not using it. Instead, I stuck to it. For two weeks I listened to them make fun of the music.

The third week the students came in and started singing to the music. I smiled and sang along. The fourth week the students entered the room, sang with the music, and some started to dance. Again, I joined in. The fifth week the students came in the room and the music was not playing. The students complained!

The message of this chapter is simple: Make music an important part of your classroom.

TEXT MESSAGE

Remember these points:
- Music changes the brains of both you and your students.
- Music makes memories of events, people, and content.
- Music can manage the movement in your classroom.

To put this information about music into a broader context, look again at the research on the arts presented in Chapter 2.

CHAPTER 9

Visual Tools

In his book *Brain Rules*, John Medina (2008) tells us that "visual processing doesn't just assist in the perception of our world. It dominates the perception of our world" (p. 224). You are able to read this book because of a brain area called the visual cortex, located at the back of your head. Your brain not only enables you to read; it also adds assumptions about what you read and what you see. The Net Generation has grown up learning how to read visual images. As a result, their visual systems are much more reflexive and intuitive about what they see. They simply learn better with visuals.

Creating a visual representation of nonlinear ideas can help students reach higher levels of thinking and access some seemingly nonrelated chunks of information in their brains. Mind mapping is one way of creating such visual representations. According to the University of Minnesota Digital Center (n.d.), the brain can process 36,000 visual images every hour.

INSTANT MESSAGE

The Net Generation and Generation Next can easily follow their digital dreams by creating mind maps using technology tools. Software such as Inspiration, the University of Minnesota Digital Center's own tool (available at http://dmc.umn.edu/objects/mindmap), and even tools like Microsoft Publisher can do the job.

The What, Why, and How of Mind Maps

Tony Buzan originated mind mapping in England in the 1970s; Michael Gelb developed it further; and Nancy Margulies learned his techniques and devised what she calls mindscapes. All of these gifted people have written wonderful books about this concept that I recommend highly. These books include Tony Buzan's *Mind Mapping*, Nancy Margulies's *Mapping Inner Space*, and Michael Gelb's *How to Think Like Leonardo da Vinci*.

What

Mind maps are graphic representations of material (See Figure 9.1 for a simple example). They hold information in a fashion that is similar to how the brain holds information, scattered in different areas. Each area is a thought or representation of a bit of information. When the bits are put together, you have the whole idea. Problem solving may be encouraged or enhanced by mind maps because they can make abstract ideas concrete.

A mind map can hold large amounts of information; but keep in mind the age of the student you are teaching and begin by keeping the maps relatively small. Some mind maps are visually attractive, but one does not need to be a great artist to create a very efficient map.

Why

Why use mind maps? Mind maps give the learner the ability to easily and quickly visualize the material being taught. The single most powerful element in memory is visual memory. By adding the emotion that is connected to each picture or symbol in the mind map, what is produced will be retained in the long-term memory bank

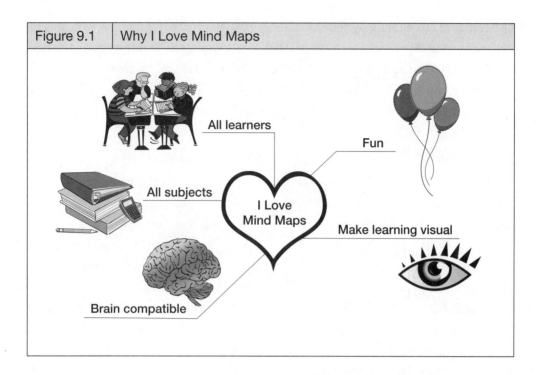

Figure 9.1 | Why I Love Mind Maps

of the brain. With mind maps, we are creating pictures that will enable the student to remember 80 to 100 percent of what we have taught. If it sounds too good to be true, consider the following facts about mind maps. Mind maps

• Are arrangements of ideas that can be linked to each other and to information already in the brain.
• Access both the left and right sides of the brain.
• Appeal to all learners starting at about age 5.
• Can have new ideas added to them quickly and easily.
• Are helpful in all subject areas.
• Are fun and easy to create.

How

Mind maps require just a few simple materials to create. You can use an interactive whiteboard, overhead, chalkboard, or flip chart and colored markers or chalk to demonstrate how to create a mind map. Students will need blank paper and markers. To effectively teach students how to create mind maps, you should set aside some time on two or three days. Approximately 30 minutes for the first session should be sufficient. No matter what grade level you teach, the same basic procedure applies. The difference is in how you set the stage for the lesson. Here are suggested procedures for lower grades and upper grades.

Lower Grades Day 1

Step 1: "How many of you like to draw? I am going to read you a short story. When I am finished, I will give you some paper and markers. I want you to draw a picture of one thing from the story that will help you remember the whole story."

Step 2: Read a very short story to the students, showing them no pictures. Pass out the materials and give them several minutes to draw a picture. If they are capable of writing a word or short phrase to go with the picture, have them do so.

Step 3: When the students have finished drawing their pictures, use a chalkboard, a whiteboard, or a sheet of paper on a bulletin board to do the following. In the center write the title of the story and put a cloud shape or circle around it. Draw lines outward from it in spiderlike fashion. Then, take the students' pictures and tape them on the board at the ends of the lines.

Step 4: Taking into account that you may have several duplicate pictures, ask one of the students to explain the story using the pictures as clues. You may then want to put the pictures in order of sequence. If there are gaps in the story, talk about what pictures might go in those gaps.

Lower Grades Day 2

Step 1: "Today we are going to make another mind map. I'll do the drawing on the overhead (chalkboard, whiteboard). The mind map will be a story about me. I'm going to call it 'My Day.'" (This idea comes from *Mapping Inner Space* by Nancy Margulies [2002].) Write "My Day" in the center of the overhead in color and draw a circle or cloud shape around it (see Figure 9.2).

Step 2: Draw a line from the center and say, "The lines that I draw here are called power lines because they connect us to the word and picture that are going to give us the power to remember. On the first line I will put the words 'wake up.' What kind of picture could I put with that word?" You may have to suggest something simple, like the sun.

Figure 9.2	Mind Map with Student Pictures

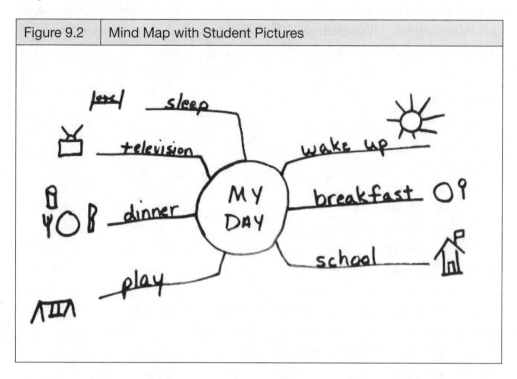

Step 3: Continue around the picture with as many lines as are necessary to complete it. Save this picture.

General rules to follow include

- Use a different color for each line.
- Use the same color for the line, word, and picture that goes with it.
- Draw the lines as horizontally as possible so that the word is written in such a way that the paper does not need to be turned to read it.

Lower Grades Day 3

Step 1: "Today we are going to make a mind map. We are going to see how well we remember. I will draw on the overhead, and you see if you can tell me exactly what was in the mind map I drew yesterday." At this point allow the children to help you recreate "My Day." Compare this picture with yesterday's picture. Applaud the excellent results!

Step 2: Now you want to allow the students time to make their own mind map. Decide on a subject you want them to use. While you stand at the board or overhead, they will each create their own mind map using large paper and markers. The first several times you do mind maps it is best to walk the students through the steps.

Step 3: Later in the day have the students re-create their mind maps. Check them against the originals. Notice if there are certain colors or sections of the paper that they forget. This is a good way to discover what individual brains find easy or difficult to remember. For instance, some people have difficulty remembering anything in the lower left-hand corner. That space should remain blank on their mind maps. Others may have difficulty remembering certain colors. (For example, I have never understood why I forget pastel colors even though I like them so much.)

Upper Grades Day 1

Step 1: "Raise your hand if you would like to have more power over your life and remember 85 to 100 percent of what you learn. If you could learn your school stuff better and study faster, would you be willing to spend a few minutes for the next few days learning this very powerful technique?"

Step 2: "Who can finish the following saying: 'A picture is worth _____.' That's right: 'a thousand words.'" Discuss for a few moments what this quote means. Ask for ways that this is true. Use television and perhaps music videos as examples.

Step 3: "If this information is correct, then wouldn't it be easier to take the material you learn at school and get a picture of it in your mind to remember it? I'm about to teach you a technique that was developed in Europe and is being used in this country because it is so powerful. What's really neat about it is that you get to draw and do just a minimum of writing to capture key ideas."

Steps 4 through 6: Follow the same procedures as outlined in the section for Lower Grades Day 2 (Steps 1 through 3) to make a mind map entitled "My Day," identifying the "power lines," asking for suggestions for pictures, and following the same general rules. Save the picture.

As simple as mind mapping seems, remember that this is a new concept for most of your students. They need you to model it several times before they own it.

Upper Grades Day 2

Steps 1 through 3: "Today we are going to re-create the mind map we made yesterday. We are going to see how well we remember." Follow the same procedures as outlined for Lower Grades Day 3 (Steps 1 through 3), re-creating the earlier mind map, comparing it with the earlier version, and then having the students create their own mind maps. If it is the beginning of the year, it is a good idea to have them do mind maps of the table of contents of their textbook. The activity provides great pre-exposure, and they get an idea of what is to come. Your students who like to see "the big picture" will appreciate this exercise.

Step 4: As described for the lower grades, check the students' re-created mind maps against the originals to see if they forget certain colors or sections of the paper. Also be aware that some students may find that they don't need the pictures or symbols. Some may find they don't need words. I strongly suggest that you insist they use both words and either symbols or pictures for the first few months that they try this strategy. After they fully understand it, they may make choices on how to use mind mapping for their personal needs.

Mind Mapping as One Choice Among Many

It is important to be aware that mind mapping may not suit all of your students. Those who are very linear-sequential in their learning may still prefer an outline. By introducing mind mapping, you are simply giving your students a choice.

A meta-analysis by Marzano, Pickering, and Pollack (2001) shows that nonlinguistic representations are one way to improve student achievement. Nonlinguistic representations are a way of imaging information, but they do not have to be in picture form. In fact, nonlinguistic representation may use any of the senses. Students may represent their learning through movement, pictures, sounds, and smells. It is more likely that they will choose movement or pictures, and those pictures may be in the form of graphic organizers, drawings, or mind maps.

The dual-coding theory expresses the idea that the brain stores knowledge in both a word form and a picture form. By actively encouraging students to create nonlinguistic representations, we may be encouraging more neural activity in the brain. In general, most teachers present information linguistically through reading or talking. Yet, according to Ruby Payne (1998), who is known for her work on teaching children of poverty, if students can't draw what they know, they really don't know it.

The Importance of Visualization

Mind maps and other nonlinguistic representations are useful for helping students visualize material that is new or difficult for them to create mental pictures of. Many strong visual learners love to create a mind map, and once they complete it, they never refer to it again. The information stays with them after it is in visual form.

The importance of teaching students how to create mental pictures cannot be overstated. In fact, according to something called the "pictorial superiority effect," if information is presented with visual imagery, it will be better remembered. After 72 hours information that is presented verbally has a recall rate of only about 10 percent. When a picture is added, the percentage goes up to 65 percent (Medina, 2008).

Here are some visual rules to remember:

- The brain pays attention to color.
- The brain pays attention to size.
- The brain pays attention to orientation.
- The brain pays attention to movement.

This information tells me as a teacher and a presenter that animations will get participants' attention. I began adding animations to my PowerPoint presentations, and it did make a difference. I began using more visuals and a bit less verbiage in my communication.

Helping Students Visualize

"Now, I want you to close your eyes and picture in your mind what I am going to describe," the 1st grade teacher said to her class. They were going to do a writing assignment based on what they pictured as she spoke. All of the 1st graders closed their eyes. She described the scene she wanted them to picture in a slow and deliberate manner. When she finished, she asked, "Would anyone like to tell me what they saw in their mind?" Antonio, from the back of the class yelled out, "Black. I just saw black!"

Antonio is not alone. Some students have more trouble visualizing than others. It often takes several repetitions of a description or a poem to get them started "seeing" pictures. Here are some steps you might want to follow:

- Read aloud a short prose selection or a poem that is very descriptive. For the first reading just have students listen to the words.
- Read the selection a second time, ask them to think about what it means, and allow them to discuss their thoughts.
- For the third reading, ask them to make a picture in their minds of what the selection means.
- Have them find a partner and share with each other the pictures they have conjured up.
- Give them a copy of the selection to take to their seats. There they can read it again and draw the picture that they see.

This strategy works well for lower grades, but I found that many of my middle school students had trouble visualizing. Their skills improved when I used the steps listed here, including drawing, which they loved to do.

TEXT MESSAGE

You may already be teaching your students mapping. The work of David Hyerle in this area is superb. After having done some work with visual thinking maps, I believe they can also make a difference in the brain. They tend to prime the brain for the type of learning it is going to do. Visual thinking maps are more specific than mind maps. The general concept is that students are taught to use specific kinds of maps when looking for specific types of data. One example is bubble maps for comparing and contrasting. For more information, read David Hyerle's book *Visual Tools for Constructing Knowledge* or visit www.thinkingmaps.com/htthinkmap.php3.

If you prefer a visual tutorial on mind mapping, YouTube has several. You'll find an introduction to the topic by Tony Buzan at www.youtube.com/watch?v=MlabrWv25qQ.

CHAPTER 10

Flashbulbs and Flash Drives: Understanding How Memory Works

When discussing memory and the brain, it's useful to think in terms of analogies—namely, flashbulbs and flash drives. A "flashbulb memory" is a memory that is created as a result of a personal event. It is usually a combination of several memory systems becoming activated at the same time. Our memory of September 11 is a flashbulb memory. The emotions associated with the event cause us to say, "I remember where I was when those planes crashed into the towers." Thinking of the location brings forth details of the event and of what we were doing at the time, and it may call forth pertinent semantic details that led up to the event and occurred after the event.

A flash drive is a small portable device for storing computer files. The drive can be erased and new information can be stored on it. Often flash drives are used to transport information from one computer to another. The only way a flash drive memory is transferred to the brain is by learning the material that is to be stored. In other words, conscious effort must be made to transfer the information.

Digital natives feel that it is not necessary to remember information when it is at our fingertips through computer files and Web sites. According to some estimates, the amount of information available is doubling each year, so the digital natives may have a point. What is worth storing in our brains? For years it was said that knowing information isn't important—it's knowing where to find it. Guess what? We now know where to find it.

Ideally, dates, statistics, and other highly specific knowledge need not be "memorized" unless the purpose of doing so is directly related to our career or is important to know for other reasons. Those of us in education, however, know that state testing and college admissions testing require our students to have a fair amount of prior knowledge. So we must continue to address issues related to memory: how it works, how to make it work better, and what is important enough to store in long-term memory.

"My students can't remember anything. They really have bad memories. What can I do?" I hear this often at workshops and conferences when I am speaking about memory. My usual answer is "baloney." No offense to anyone; I know we have students with memory problems. But if you take a close look at the amount of new knowledge our students have acquired, you might agree with me.

Through the use of their techno-toys, they have developed their own language. They have excellent memories for the things they want to remember. Consider the following list of abbreviations and their meanings:

- BTW = by the way
- BFN = bye for now
- BRB =be right back
- FYI = for your information
- FWIW = for what it's worth
- IM(H)O = in my (humble) opinion
- ROFL = rolling on the floor laughing
- TIA or TA = thanks in advance
- LOL = laughing out loud
- TTYL = talk to you later
- TIFN = that's it for now

This list is just a small sampling. The bottom line is this: your students learn what they want or need to learn. Learning and remembering the content you present may be a matter of making that content desirable. The survival brain is interested in one of two things: desire and need. The questions the brain asks when presented with new information are "Do I need to know this information?" and "Do I want to know this information?"

What do our students need? I have asked students at different grade levels what it is that people their ages need. We did a "Top 10" list in the manner of David Letterman. Figure 10.1 shows the consensus from different grade levels and from multiple classes at each of those levels.

Figure 10.1	Students' Top 10 Needs	
Grade 3	**Grade 6**	**Grade 10**
10. Wii	10. Bicycle	10. MySpace
9. Friends	9. Family	9. Freedom
8. Money	8. Shelter	8. Friends
7. Shelter	7. Food	7. Xbox
6. Food	6. Money	6. Sex
5. Family	5. Xbox	5. HDTV
4. Laptop/Internet	4. Boyfriend/Girlfriend	4. Laptop
3. Xbox	3. HDTV	3. Money
2. HDTV	2. Laptop	2. Cell phone
1. Cell phone	1. Cell phone	1. Car

Please notice that the following were not on the lists: math, reading, science, social studies, spelling, history, or foreign language. In fact, these were not included when I asked the students to do a Top 20 list. Need I say more? My point is this: if we can only get information into the brain that students believe they either need or want, then our content area information will be accepted by the brain only if we present it in a desirable way. We must make students *want* to learn if they don't think they *need* to learn! Understanding how memory works will assist us in this endeavor.

Improving Memory by Using Memory

I download my brain every day. That sounds crazy! What am I downloading? I download my short-term memories: immediate memory and working memory. Where do I download them? Onto my computer, or my smart phone, or my iPod, or just a piece of paper? Why do I do it? I am emptying my short-term memory to make space for new information. Having too much information stored in temporary memory keeps me from retrieving information and storing new information.

If your students are not downloading these fragile bits of information, you will see the consequences in their assessments. As I stated in my first book on memory (Sprenger, 1999), memory is the only evidence we have of learning. Cognitive overload, sensory overload, or short-term memory overload are all the same phenomenon: in a space that is meant for five to seven bits of information, the eighth bit is either not going in or it's pushing another bit out. Consider the following example.

Madonna has just read the homework assignment posted on the bulletin board by the classroom door as she heads to her next class. Her lips move as she repeats the assignment over and over until she can get it written down or commit it to memory. "Read pages 85 to 89, answer the odd-number questions on the bottom of page 89, and draw a map of Australia," she says over and over.

Just as she is about to enter her math class, her friend Kiersten grabs Madonna's arm and shouts, "Don't forget about tonight! We have to bake 24 cupcakes and 45 cookies for the book fair tomorrow. Meet at my house at 7:15."

Madonna nods and adds this information to her list. "Read pages 85 to 89—or was it 45 to 85? No, that's too much. Answer the questions at the bottom of page 24. And how many cupcakes? 89? Yes, that's it." She dashes to her desk, pulls out some paper, and starts writing her information down: "45 cupcakes, 85 cookies, read pages 24 to 36. 36? I'm not sure I remember that number." She is about to give up, but instead she pulls out her cell phone. She sends a text message to Kiersten asking what time they're supposed to meet and what they need to bake. Then Madonna gets on the Internet, goes to her social studies home page, and looks up the assignment. Mrs. Castle hasn't posted it yet, so she will have to check again later. She calls her home phone and leaves herself a message on the answering machine reminding herself to check the Web site to get her assignment. Just as she finishes, she sees Mr. Robinson walking toward her, shaking his head. She turns off her cell phone and puts it in her book bag before he reaches her desk.

We are bombarded with information. Emotion-laden messages come at us quickly, and our brains must decide what to pay attention to and what to drop. Memory is fragile. But in this case, Madonna had some technology to help her out. One of the many dilemmas facing educators today is this: Do we rely too heavily on technology assistance? Are we underutilizing our memory power by writing things down?

Short-Term Memory Processes

There are three short-term memory processes: sensory memory, immediate memory, and working memory. Each plays a different role and is associated with different parts of the brain.

Sensory Memory

All sensory information except for our sense of smell enters our brains through the brain stem. (Smell has a more direct route, and the olfactory center in the brain is very close to the areas associated with emotion. This may be why smells bring back memories instantly, and they usually have an emotional component to them.) This sensory information is sorted and sent to the appropriate brain areas to be examined. For instance, visual information is sent to the occipital lobe for visual processing. Sensory memory has a span of about four seconds to either be dropped or to be held a bit longer in immediate memory. Some researchers call this sensory system "buffers."

Immediate Memory

If information is found to be useful, the process of immediate memory begins. Immediate memory holds information for 15 to 30 seconds. This is the memory we use to look up a number in the phone book. We hold the number in memory until we enter it on our phone. Then it quickly disappears.

Madonna was facing this type of situation. If she had had the time to write down her assignment, she may have had no dilemma at all. She would have been able to drop the assignment information from her immediate memory and instead hold on to the baking information without a problem. Instead, the two chunks of information became enmeshed in her brain and she had to take a little more time to sort things out.

Immediate memory has not only a time limit, but also a load limit. Researchers have discovered that the processing power for short-term memory begins with space for one bit of information at the age of 3. Then, every other year we get power for another space until about age 15, when we have memory space for seven items.

If we have space for seven items, why did Madonna have so much trouble? At her age, she hasn't developed the processing power of an adult. She may also have fewer memory strategies to use or other information may have been taking up space in her immediate memory.

Working Memory

This type of short-term memory is a process that takes place in the prefrontal cortex and the temporal lobes of the brain. It is sometimes called a "scratch pad." It is here, with the help of the hippocampus, that we rehearse new information and combine it with previously stored knowledge. If we take information from immediate memory and spend time thinking about it, rehearsing it, combining it with other things we know, we are maximizing this process of working memory. Making connections and making sense to ourselves allows the information to become a long-term memory.

We have all probably used working memory in other ways. As a student I can recall waiting until the last moment to study for an exam. I would stay up most of the night cramming. This strategy involves repetition and rehearsal. It usually does not involve trying to make any real connections or real sense of the material. Minutes before the test I might still be studying my notes. I would dash into the classroom and beg for the test paper right away, knowing that I was about to forget vital answers. Fortunately for my grade point average, this technique was somewhat successful. I would pass the test and sometimes do quite well. But the moment I walked out of that classroom, my brain dumped most of that information.

Recent research suggests that improving working memory capacity can improve achievement (Klingberg, 2008). The question is, how do we increase working memory? Practice. Challenging practice. Although some educators feel this is a waste of precious time, perhaps we should take a closer look at the research. Improvement in working memory was seen only when children worked at the limits of their capacity and on a regular basis.

Because our students do not need to memorize phone numbers and other bits of data, they have gotten out of the habit of using their memories. Most of you remember memorizing poems, preambles, and short pieces of text in school. It is this kind of challenge activity, along with mental math problems, that can make a difference.

Long-Term Memory

The process of taking information and storing it for long periods of time is called long-term memory. There are those who believe that we have a lifetime of long-term memories stored that are just waiting to be accessed. Brain researchers believe that after a period of time these memories are no longer available. Still others are certain that we replace our old memories with new ones. Consider the following examples:

> The students enter the classroom where their home economics teacher has begun creating the base for a marinara sauce that they will all be making as part of Italian cooking week. Marguerite strolls in talking to her friends, but she stops quickly, sniffs the air, and says, "I remember how my grandma used to make lasagna for us. It smells just like her house in here."
>
> The music teacher tells her students that they will be singing the school song at the assembly after school today. The boys and girls look at her in shock. "We never learned that song," Sara says. As Mrs. Murphy begins playing the melody on the piano, the students remember the song and begin to practice.
>
> Some former students return to school to visit after graduating several years ago. As they walk in, Sondra says, "I can't remember anything that happened here. I guess I didn't like it much." As the group walks down the hall, Sondra suddenly blurts out, "This is where we had to line up and prepare for a tornado! And that is the room where Mr. Little, the science teacher, had a small explosion and ruined his tie! I guess I do have memories from school!"

Each of these experiences demonstrates part of the wonder of long-term memory. Each was triggered in a different manner, illustrating part of the mystery of memory. Some of our memories are decades old, but with the right stimulus it seems as though the remembered events happened only yesterday.

With current brain-imaging techniques it is possible to see how and where memories are stored. Keep in mind that memories are not stored in one location in the brain. Your memory of your first day at school is divided into different regions in the brain. When you recall the memory, you actually piece it back together in working memory.

The Brain's Memory Systems

The brain has different memory systems that are activated by dissimilar types of triggers or cues. The systems include semantic, episodic, emotional, procedural, and conditioned response memory (Sprenger, 2005). What is stored in one system is not necessarily stored in another. We can compare the memory systems to aisles in the grocery store. I can spend all day walking up and down the bread aisle, but I'm never going to find the butter there. If we can't remember something, the reason may be that the correct trigger for that memory system has not presented itself. In my classroom I like to keep these systems in mind to help students learn and remember more easily.

Semantic Memory

Semantic memory holds information we have learned from words. Our educational system relies heavily on semantic memory. Textbooks and lectures give us semantic information, but retention of this information is poor until we have had enough engagements with the material.

New information enters the brain through the brain stem, goes to the thalamus, and is sent to the hippocampus, which is the file cabinet for our factual memories. Just as the aisles at the market have signs that tell us what items are on those shelves, the hippocampus has signs or files for our memories. If incoming sensory information is factual, it triggers the hippocampus to search its files for matching information. The hippocampus brings information into those short-term buffers to be examined. If the stored information connects to the new information, the new information is sent to the prefrontal cortex for working memory to take over. Working memory will continue to sort and sift the old and new material. Through prior knowledge or interest, the new information may be added to the old to form more long-term memory. This process may have to be repeated several times before long-term memory is formed.

The semantic memory system is a difficult system to use for learning. Several repetitions of the learning are required to cement it into the memory system. The learning has to be stimulated by associations, comparisons, and similarities. In short, semantic memory can fail us in many ways.

Despite its drawbacks, semantic memory has some good points. The hippocampus has access to a wealth of files just waiting to be opened. It also has an unlimited capacity to help the cortex of the brain store new information. The proper associations can open up any of those files and remind you of the factual information that you have stored.

INSTANT MESSAGE

 The hippocampus is a small structure. If too much information is sent to it in a short period of time, some information may not be stored.

Net Gen students aren't very interested in storing information in their brains. They prefer to use their digital devices for storage. Many of us have fallen victim to this preference. For instance, I don't know my daughter's home phone number. It's speed dial #3 on my cell phone, and it's also programmed into my home phone. (While writing this book I confessed to my daughter that I didn't know her home phone number "by heart." She announced that she had all of our phone numbers stored in her brain. That made me feel a bit guilty until she told me that the contact list on her phone had become inaccessible for a few weeks and she was forced to learn the numbers! Memorizing has become a survival skill.)

Our students know how quickly they can access information when they need it. The state assessments, however, don't allow them to use digital devices. Somehow, some of the information we teach them has to make connections in their brains and become long-term memories. Manipulating information online, on their iPods, and on their phones does represent rehearsal of the material, and in time permanent memories may be formed, but relying on these methods is insufficient.

Episodic Memory

Episodic memory deals with locations, events, and people. It has sometimes been called contextual or spatial memory. The important link for this memory system is that you are always *somewhere* when you learn something. That learning may easily be associated with the location. As with semantic memory, the gateway to the episodic memory system is the hippocampus. Remember that the hippocampus stores all factual information and location is factual information. It is almost as though this brain area has two file drawers, one for semantic memories and the other for episodic memories.

A frequently used example of episodic memory applies to those of us who are old enough to remember when President Kennedy was shot. We may ask each other, "Where were you when you found out about the assassination of J.F.K.?" Younger people may relate better to the death of Michael Jackson. These memories fall into the "flashbulb" category I mentioned at the beginning of this chapter.

The point is that we all remember some information because it is related to a location. When you are learning how to drive, the car that you learn in will be easier for you to drive than other cars. Even though most cars are designed similarly, you will remember the instructions that you received and associate them with that particular car. Taking your driving test in another car will make the experience more difficult.

Many studies have demonstrated the importance of episodic memory. Students who learn information in one room and are tested in another consistently underperform (Sprenger, 20005). This occurs because episodic memory has an important component that can be called "invisible information." Students have more trouble solving math problems in English class than they do in their math class. Why? The walls, desks, overheads, chalkboards, and even the math teacher are covered with invisible information. The content of the room becomes part of the context of the memory.

Does a digital episode of learning have the same effect on the brain? Our digital natives take virtual tours, converse with people on the other side of the world, and share their learning on a blog. Are these experiences as memorable as the "real" thing? Probably not. We learn two ways: through an actual experience or by connecting new information to old information already stored in the brain (Wolfe, 2001).

An in-person experience related to new concepts will lead to a stronger memory of those concepts than reading about them online or in a text. However, if students have some background knowledge, they may be able to make connections in various ways that will help them remember the material.

Events are also part of episodic memory. The interaction that students have as they work together on projects and products may be quite memorable. When students work in dyads or small groups, the experience, along with the information, may become a strong episodic memory. If the students' emotions are also involved, the memory becomes even stronger as the formation of emotional memories is strengthened through specific brain chemicals.

Procedural Memory

The procedural memory system has often been called "muscle memory." Information found in this system deals with processes that your body does and remembers, such as your ability to ride a bike, skip rope, roller skate, ski, and, after you have perfected the task, drive a car.

The part of your brain that stores this information is called the cerebellum. For years it was thought that this brain structure was used solely for balance and posture. But recent research suggests that the cerebellum does much more, including storing any procedure that becomes routine.

When you first learned to drive, not only was your episodic memory storing information; your procedural memory was also activated. The sequence used in driving was stored in this memory system. The procedures of stopping at a red light, hitting the brakes when you see the brake lights of the car in front of you, and turning the steering wheel to round corners and avoid collisions are all stored here. Sometimes you can trigger procedural memory by getting into the same position and doing whatever you were doing at the time. For example, many people have easier times remembering something they learned while standing up if they just stand up to trigger the memory.

Digital natives follow procedures when they're using computers and other digital devices. Will this kind of procedure trigger a procedural memory? It would seem that only a novel procedure would create such a memory. The brain habituates easily to repetitive tasks. When Germaine creates a PowerPoint presentation on quadratic equations for his math class, does the sequence of steps he uses to create the presentation help him remember the content? Quite possibly, but there is more than procedural memory at work. Choosing the background for his presentation may access episodic memory, as might the location where he created the PowerPoint presentation. As he practices his presentation, he may experience positive feelings of accomplishment if he feels he knows the material and is doing a good job, or negative feelings if he continually makes mistakes. Both of these situations may access emotional memories that will be attached to the material. The very act of teaching others will also activate different memory systems in Germaine: semantic memory from the practice and repetition, emotional memory from the act of presenting to his peers, episodic memory from the location and the people present, and emotional memory again as he receives feedback from his teacher and classmates.

Conditioned Response Memory

The conditioned response memory system is also located in the cerebellum. I call this type of memory "automatic memory" because the remembered information is automatically triggered by certain stimuli, such as a song that is playing. Once the first few words are sung or right after you hear the opening notes, you begin to sing the song.

What might you have stored in automatic memory? In addition to a lot of songs, the alphabet is there, along with the multiplication tables and probably your ability to decode words. That means that your ability to read (but not your ability to comprehend) is located in your cerebellum. Sets of words are also stored here: *stop and go*, *black and white*, *up and down*, *in and out*. If you practiced learning information on flashcards, that material would be remembered in your automatic memory. Any learning that has become automatic for you could be stored in your automatic memory.

Your automatic memory can cause other memory systems to open. For instance, you hear a song on the radio that you haven't heard in a long time. You begin to sing the song. As you are singing, you remember the last time you sang that song. Your episodic memory has been triggered. You picture yourself clutching the steering wheel of your blue Oldsmobile as you wound around the hill. You have activated your procedural memory. As you think about the car, you recall fond memories of you and your friends. Your semantic system has opened up with this factual information.

Emotional Memory

Your emotional memory system is opened through the amygdala. This brain structure is located in the limbic brain, next to the hippocampus. While the hippocampus catalogs factual information, the amygdala catalogs emotional information. This filing cabinet is filled with files containing all sorts of experiences that made you happy or sad or experience any other feeling you can name.

A key point to remember about emotional memory is that it takes precedence over any other kind of memory. The brain always gives priority to your emotions. When information enters your brain and reaches your thalamus, your amygdala will grab that information if it is emotional and go straight to work on it. If the information elicits strong emotion, especially fear, the amygdala takes over to prepare your body. Daniel Goleman (1996) calls this response a "neural hijacking." At this point, no other memory systems have a chance.

The stress response may be employed by the amygdala and cause all sorts of havoc. The release of stress hormones such as cortisol may cause interrupted transmission of information in your brain and make it impossible to think clearly. All of the memory systems could be blocked by these unwanted and sometimes dangerous chemicals.

Your emotional memory may be triggered by another memory system, and then it may take over your "logical" mind. For instance, suppose you need to do some research for a project. You think to yourself that you must make time to visit the local library to look at some original documents in the archives. Suddenly, as you picture the library through your semantic memory system, you "see" in your mind the librarian, who is someone you cannot tolerate. Your anger and disgust take over your thinking. You may then decide to go to a different library, forget the research, or simply go to the library and try to avoid her. Your choice will depend on how strong your feelings are.

Strategies for Triggering Memory Systems

The following strategies for triggering the various memory systems are simply suggestions. You may have or develop others that work for you.

- Semantic
  - Mnemonic devices
  - Summaries
  - Mind maps
  - Pictures

- Episodic
  - Change in seating arrangement
  - Use of colored paper, pens, or chalk
  - Field trips
  - Accessories

- Procedural
  - Puppet shows
  - Action figures
  - Dance
  - Manipulatives

- Conditioned Response (automatic)
  - Flash cards
  - Limericks
  - Metaphors
  - Songs

- Emotional
  - Humor
  - Stories
  - Music
  - Celebrations

Digital Strategies

Your students may be used to storing, filing, and retrieving information through their high-tech tools. Offer them choices for working with information digitally and nondigitally. First, it may be worked with on a computer, and after it is rehearsed in many ways, it may be stored as long-term memories in their brains instead of just on their computer hard drives.

According to research, students may need to be engaged with a new concept 28 times over a three-week period to get the information stored permanently (Marzano, Pickering, & Pollack, 2001). Technology offers multiple ways of engaging students with the material. Here are some suggestions:

- Semantic
  - Mind maps
  - Blogging
  - Texting
  - Searching online

- Episodic
  - Story searches
  - Use of computer lab setting

- Procedural
  - Software programs with step-by-step instructions
  - PowerPoint presentations
  - Organizational routines
  - Programs with drag-and-drop features

- Automatic
  - Memory games
  - Computerized flashcards
  - Creating poetry using software or online resources

- Emotional
  - Blogging
  - Texting
  - Group computer time

TEXT MESSAGE

Remember these key points about the relationship between memories, experience, background knowledge, and new information:

- Memories are made from our experiences.
- Experiences provide background knowledge.
- Background knowledge allows us to find places in our brain to store new information.
- New information provides more background knowledge.
- More background knowledge provides the brain with more connections that additional concepts, understandings, and facts can be attached to.

Memories make us smarter and give us the tools to be creative, to synthesize, and to build relationships. These are 21st century skills that our students need to succeed.

PART 4

Balancing Digital Desires with Digital Natives' Needs

Finding balance in the 21st century is no easy task. This section explores strategies for helping our students learn and relearn how to deal with people face-to-face as well as meeting their technological needs. Many are asking, "What will our students need to know?" and "What will learning be like in the future?" To find answers, we explore online learning and schools that give students the gift of time.

CHAPTER 11

The Balancing Act

High school students John and Jarrett are real go-getters when it comes to innovative ideas involving technology. Together they worked on creating wikis for each class in the history, English, and math departments. John and Jarrett created a slide presentation to show the teachers how the wikis would work. The teachers used the wikis to help other students organize group projects. The wikis saved classroom time that students would have otherwise needed for planning, and they allowed the teachers to check up on what each team was planning.

The wikis were so good that the associate superintendent in charge of technology called John and Jarrett into her office. She had spoken with some businesses in the community about having the boys present their ideas to them. These were businesses that had partnerships with the school, and Mrs. Mercer thought this would be a wonderful opportunity for the district to reciprocate the support these businesses had given them.

The boys were excited as they headed off the next day to present their ideas to a room full of business managers, most of whom were in their 40s and 50s ("digital immigrants" in the technology world). Despite the positive anticipation on both sides, the results of the meeting were disappointing.

Mr. Caldwell stood up to shake hands with John and Jarrett and to introduce the boys to the other attendees. John fumbled with his laptop and backpack before he finally freed his right hand to shake. Jarrett was busy setting up the projector and connecting to the Internet and never even noticed the handshake. He completely missed the introductions.

Right from the start, the managers had lots of questions, but the boys told them that the presentation would answer their questions. The slide presentation was very creative and included some video, music, and voice, but there was little eye contact between John and Jarrett and their audience, and their comments were limited to a few "uh-huhs." The business people had more questions after the slide show, but John and Jarrett's responses were brief, stilted, and seemed unfriendly. At the end of the meeting, the managers left feeling disinterested and disappointed. Mr. Caldwell called Mrs. Mercer after the boys' departure and explained that the boys and the business people hadn't connected. He couldn't quite put his finger on it, but there just didn't seem to be a fit between the boys' ideas and the organizations' needs.

This incident is not a highly unusual occurrence when it comes to interactions between digital natives and digital immigrants. The boys had lost or never developed the social skills that would have encouraged anticipation and excitement in their possible clients. The deficiency is important, and we need to be aware of it as we educate our students, because connecting to people on a social-emotional level is going to be crucial in dealing with 21st century organizations.

Competition is fierce and knowledge workers are easily available. If information is all that organizations require, it's easy to obtain. Work can be outsourced to other countries where wages and the cost of living are lower.

Daniel Pink (2005) reminds us that the world needs highly creative people with strong interpersonal skills. As mentioned in Chapter 1, he calls for us to educate our students in ways that will help them to develop "high-concept" skills—the ability to detect patterns, to connect unrelated ideas, and to create something new. They also need to develop "high-touch" skills—the ability to empathize, to read faces and gestures, and to find joy in themselves and bring it out in others.

The Digital World and Social-Emotional Intelligence

Technology makes it easy to lose the human touch. Students feel connected to each other through their words and acronyms transmitted via instant messages and texting, but if it weren't for emoticons smiling, frowning, and winking at the end of a message, they wouldn't be certain if the message was serious or silly.

Dealing with people on a face-to-face level requires practice. Baby boomers remember playing outside with friends, interacting with family, and just people watching. Through these activities they learned what people said, how they said it, and how their bodies moved when they spoke, which added meaning to the speech. These cues told us how to respond appropriately.

Whether we are using technology in the classroom or not, social-emotional intelligence is an area that is vital to a brain-compatible classroom. As students rely more on high-tech equipment to communicate, we may have to reteach some face-to-face skills as well as fine-tune their written communication skills. An e-mail I received from a former student illustrates this need:

> Dear Mrs. Sprenger,
>
> I find it interesting that you have decided to write a book about digital media to teachers. Good luck with that! Let's face it; the ability to handle new technology is practically innate to young people. By writing this book are you telling teachers that you are intellectually superior to them? Or is it that I am especially clever and intellectually superior? Perhaps, I was born with a better-quality brain.
>
> I will look forward to reading your book.
> Your former student,
> Evan

I was totally stumped as to the meaning of this correspondence. Was Evan mad at me? He was a pretty good student who occasionally got into trouble with his snide remarks, but I had thought he liked me. Was Evan being serious? Sarcastic? Funny? I forwarded the e-mail to my daughter, Marnie. Because she is a member of the Net Generation, I thought she could surely help me out. I try to respond to all of my e-mail, and I wanted to be sure to send an appropriate message in response.

Marnie read it and was equally puzzled. This is a problem with e-mail, texting, and instant messaging. In oral speech, only 7 percent of the communication is in the words (Estes, 2008). Most of the "message" comes through tone of voice and body language. When we are looking at text only, it can be very difficult to discern the exact meaning. Marnie firmly believes that emoticons—icons that convey various emotions—can make the difference.

As our students create and handle relationships through various digital media, it becomes important that they find ways to communicate their feelings. This is where emoticons come into play. Here is a list of the common ones:

:-) Smiling

:-> Sarcastic

:-(Frowning

;-) Winking

:-o Surprised

>:-< Mad

:-@ Screaming

:-S Incoherent

:-\ Undecided

:-* Oops

:'-(Crying

:-| Indifferent

If Evan had used some of these emotional signals, I would have had a better idea of what he was trying to tell me.

Dear Mrs. Sprenger,

I find it interesting that you have decided to write a book about digital media to teachers. Good luck with that! :-) Let's face it; the ability to handle new technology is practically innate to young people. By writing this book are you telling teachers that you are intellectually superior to them? :-o Or is it that I am especially clever and intellectually superior? Perhaps, I was born with a better-quality brain. ;-)

I will look forward to reading your book.

Your former student,

Evan

A smile, a surprised face, and a wink change the meaning for me. I feel free to write back to Evan in a friendly manner, and perhaps I will ask him for advice because he truly is more advanced than I am in the area of digital technology.

Years ago I had parents tell me how their shy son or daughter was finally interacting with other students in class via instant messaging and e-mail. Did I think that was wonderful? For those students who are too shy to initiate conversations with others, especially during those awkward years of adolescence, it could be a positive step. But this should not be the sum total of the child's social relationships.

Research suggests that spending too much time communicating through technology robs some of our students of their people skills. When it is time for them to work with classmates and socialize with students their own age or older, they often misread social cues. Even though our students have opportunities to gather knowledge from other students throughout the world and from various Web sites and blogs, studies recommend that students have enough personal interactions to learn to understand others' feelings and handle relationships (Small & Vorgan, 2008).

Guiding Students Toward a Healthy Balance

As educators, we can do several things to guide our students toward a healthy balance between their high-tech connectedness and their face-to-face, personal interactions. The following sections suggest several strategies to help you achieve this goal.

Balance Creativity with Technology

Creativity is the ability to produce new ideas and then implement them. Students require the experiences to build upon to spark creativity. Although we think of creative people as being spontaneously creative, the truth is that those ideas are based on background knowledge. Offering our students opportunities for creative moments comes from introducing them to others' ideas and insights.

Technology will allow students to collaborate with others in all parts of the world and gather information at a very fast pace. Brainstorming sessions can take place through blogs and conversations on Skype, but the students will still need to physically interact with materials and people. If you've ever orchestrated a brainstorming session in your classroom, you know how quickly students can bounce ideas off each other. Sometimes two students will look at each other and get that "aha" moment at the same time. Their contagious emotions play a role in their ability to connect.

We often think that kids only use their imaginations when they are out and about playing with other children. If the demise of unstructured playtime can be blamed on anything, should it be technology? Or do parents and schools need to look at the glut of organized activities in which students are involved? Technology should not be the scapegoat here. In fact, students can be imaginative and creative when playing digitally. Like anything else, moderation is key.

As I discussed in Chapter 4, giving students choices is important to their motivation, but you can create rules about how much time should be given to technology and nondigital means. As educators, we should be able to recognize creativity or lack thereof. If we find students are spending more time digitally and exhibiting less creativity, it is time to step in and suggest other forms of interaction to promote ideas.

Let's not forget though, that some very creative writers can get published or publish themselves on the Internet. Some budding authors can receive feedback from students around the globe.

Provide Time for Reflection

After searching for information, learning, or listening, give your students time to reflect and take notes. Reflection uses different areas of the brain and allows some overworked areas to get much-needed rest.

One high school teacher who had been unexpectedly asked to use a block schedule was panicked about how to use so much time in a productive way. A professional development workshop encouraged the use of journaling as an opportunity to have students think about their thinking. He took this idea and used it to accomplish a number of goals. First, the students were asked to write how they felt about the learning experience. To do this, they had to recall the learning and thus were automatically rehearsing the information. Second, he asked them to write how another class might react to this lesson—for example, what could make it better. This gave the teacher excellent feedback about who "got it" and who needed more help. Third, he asked that they offer suggestions as to what other ways they would like to study this material. This provided the teacher with fodder for differentiation. Many of the students requested learning only through digital means; however, as he tried to balance digital learning with other interactive approaches such as group work, some of them began to include more face-to-face learning activities on their lists.

Emphasize Face-to-Face Interactions

Take away the toys occasionally and let them practice focusing on real people and real experiences. One of my own favorite teachers kept a sign below the clock that read "BE HERE NOW." Talk to your students about that statement and what it means.

Have a listening time. Explain how uncomfortable it is to be conversing with someone who is reading or sending a text message. For a content-related listening activity, put students in pairs. Each student has three minutes to discuss the current topic. The partner must actively listen, maintain eye contact, and not interrupt. After both partners have spoken and listened, they discuss what was said and how the experience felt. Attentive listening usually promotes empathy and connectedness. Those students not as familiar with the material will also gain content knowledge through this listening activity. Discuss the experience as a whole class as well. Find out how the students felt about prolonged face-to-face communication. Did they notice facial expressions and body language?

Using Technical Skills Wisely

In Chapter 4, I mention respecting your students' digital brains. Letting them teach other students is a good approach. It is time, however, that we make sure that all of the educators and staff at our schools also understand what it is that the students are doing.

Digital Immigrants can consist of three different generations. Traditionalists are the oldest group in education. They have little desire to become tech savvy. Then, there are those who are of the baby boom generation. They use technology enough to get by. Not as eager to learn as the Net Geners, Boomer teachers and administrators have not kept up with the latest technology. The third generation is the early

Generation X group. They are much more attuned to what is going on in the digital world, yet they may have had little time to learn what their students know.

In addition to teaching other students what they can do digitally, give students the opportunity to help teachers get up to date. After-school programs, professional development days, and summer school can make teachers out of our students and benefit everyone. When these techy students see that they are respected and valuable to the school, they may be more motivated to please the teachers and help other students.

Engage Students' Brains with Interactive Whiteboards

Digital natives interact with their world digitally. They read blogs and comment on them. They use MySpace and Facebook to share their thoughts with friends around the world. They are accustomed to looking at screens. Interactive whiteboards create an interactive, digital setting in the classroom by allowing you to display anything that is on a computer screen—text, images, Web pages, and other information—on the whiteboard surface. Interactive whiteboards can replace traditional whiteboards, flipcharts, or overheads. They have the added benefit of allowing the user to manipulate or annotate the information on the whiteboard with a finger, a special pen, or a remote device. Students can work together at the whiteboard, or the entire class can take turns participating. Students can move and communicate with each other as they interact with technology. The images can be recorded and saved for absent students or for students who would benefit from repeated instruction. Digital natives find working with interactive whiteboards as interesting as working on their computers. Interactive whiteboards are available from several companies, and you can see instructional videos on company Web sites or on YouTube.

Build Emotional Literacy

As previously noted, many of today's students lack skills in face-to-face communication. Communicating digitally is quick and efficient with hard data, but when dealing with others, students need to be able to recognize emotion and use their emotional intelligence to help make decisions, work with others, and understand themselves. High-tech students lose their ability to read faces and body language. Since many of the futurists like Pink (2005) believe that empathy may be the key element in this new age, emotional intelligence skills must be reinforced. A meta-analysis of more than one hundred studies showed that students who had social-emotional learning performed better than those who did not. Their grades improved, achievement test scores were 14 percent higher than the control group, they were less impulsive, and they knew how to calm themselves (Lantieri, 2008). Social-emotional learning is a specific program that uses Daniel Goleman's (1996) emotional intelligence competencies: self-awareness, self-management, social awareness, and relationship management.

Including emotional awareness in the classroom can help students examine their feelings and notice how others are feeling, and it can improve their ability to read facial cues so they become more skilled in face-to-face interactions. An emotional awareness program can begin by simply providing a few moments each day for students to check to see how they are feeling.

When I took attendance in my classrooms at all levels, I asked the students to say "here" followed by a number from 1 to 10. A "1" would indicate "I feel yucky" or "I don't want to be here"; a "10" would tell me and the others that this student was feeling great and probably looking forward to the day. If the students told the truth—and sometimes they did not—I would have a pretty good idea of how much learning would take place. If a lot of students responded with low numbers, I knew they needed an opportunity to explore those feelings through journaling or talking. Once I felt that my students were more aware of their own feelings, I began giving them opportunities to become aware of others' feelings. I started with simple drawings or posters showing different facial expressions. The students would try to decide how that person was feeling. Sometimes the students paired up and took turns making faces; the partner had to guess what emotion was being expressed. After accomplishing the goal of recognizing others' feelings, we would move on to handling relationships. This would be done through role-play or by discussing real-time, real-life school experiences.

INSTANT MESSAGE

Excellent programs for social-emotional learning are available through organizations such as the Collaborative for Academic, Social, and Emotional Learning (CASEL). Go to www.casel.org for information and other resources.

Encourage Mindfulness

Mindfulness asks students to think about their thinking. It employs relaxation techniques and permits them to be connected only to themselves. Breathing and meditation techniques may help to create mindfulness and reduce stress among students.

The book *Building Emotional Intelligence* by Linda Lantieri (2008) provides techniques for encouraging mindful practice and includes a CD with exercises led by psychologist and science writer Daniel Goleman. The book is divided into grade levels, with different instructional approaches for each.

Some teachers encourage mindfulness by providing students with a time for quiet and calm. They may suggest that students choose a mantra, a sound, or a word that the student repeats silently while sitting comfortably, breathing in and out slowly. The student focuses on both the breathing and the mantra, clearing the mind of other thoughts. After spending as little as five minutes doing this, students report feeling more energized and more attentive.

Encourage High-Concept and High-Touch Aptitudes

Storytelling is an excellent way to enhance conceptual understandings and emotional connectedness. Our students are experts at finding information, but how they package that information in concepts and how they share it emotionally may be what makes them successful in the 21st century.

Storytelling is what the brain likes best. As we struggle to keep our students' digital brains more attentive in the classroom, turning to storytelling may be one means to that end. When we tell them stories, students generally give us more eye contact as they watch our gestures. They pay attention to the inflection in our voices. And if we tell a simple story that relates to them and our content on several levels, we can engage them in purposeful learning.

Malcolm Gladwell, bestselling author and a wonderful storyteller, writes about success in his book *Outliers* (2008). One of his subjects is Bill Gates, the founder of Microsoft. Digital brains would clearly be interested in the actual story of how he and other digital inventors and entrepreneurs rose to the top. But after telling her students she wanted to share some information about Bill Gates, Mrs. Lovett decided to first tell them the Aesop fable "The Tortoise and the Hare." The students listened attentively because they were curious to find the link between this silly story and Bill Gates. "The moral of the story," she began to say. "Slow and steady wins the race," Jonathon blurted out. "But what does that have to do with Bill Gates dropping out of school and becoming one of the wealthiest men in the world?" Mrs. Lovett then told the Bill Gates story that most of them didn't know and that Malcolm Gladwell had told in his book about success—the fact that Bill Gates, Michael Jordan, and the Beatles all had to put in at least 10,000 hours of work and practice to become the "overnight" successes that they were. After reflecting on this information, Mrs. Lovett and her class continued their study of inventors.

The Natives Are Restless

It may seem as though many of our students are more emotional about their technology than they are about human relationships. If you are teaching the adolescent brain, which could be the brain of anyone from age 9 or 10 through 25, you should know that there is more going on inside their brain than the love of technology. As the adolescent brain goes through the blooming and pruning stages, emotional levels are high and impulse control may be low. The prefrontal cortex in this brain needs our help in making decisions, staying on task, and moving to abstract levels. Students may feel isolated and alone as their bodies and minds go through many changes. Sometimes they find anonymity through digital means, and sometimes they make poor choices on social networks. If we stay attuned to their individual needs and understand their technology, we may be able to help them feel and be safe and secure in both the digital world and the classroom.

TEXT MESSAGE

 There are wonderful books on social-emotional learning. They include *Emotional Intelligence* (1996) by Daniel Goleman, *The Educator's Guide to Emotional Intelligence and Academic Achievement* (2006) edited by Maurice Elias and Harriet Arnold, and *Promoting Social and Emotional Learning* (1997) by Elias and colleagues. My book *Becoming a "Wiz" at Brain-Based Teaching* (Sprenger, 2006) has a chapter devoted to emotional intelligence that includes classroom activities. I would also refer you to your state standards. For example, my state of Illinois has social-emotional learning standards with suggestions for activities to do with students (see www.isbe.state.il.us/ils/social_emotional/standards.htm).

CHAPTER 12

The Present and the Future of Learning

----- 🌐 -----

There are two questions before us: *What* should we be teaching our students, many of whom may live to be 150 years old? and *How* are we going to teach our students when information is doubling every two years?

The answer to the first question is exquisitely simple, but certainly not easy. We must teach them to be lifelong learners. The fact that 50 percent of the information they learn their freshman year in college will be obsolete by the time they are seniors tells us that they must be prepared for change (Tapscott, 2009). And change is constant. They must be trainable and retrainable. Learning quickly is going to be an important skill. Being creative is going to be absolutely necessary. Our students will need to synthesize information and present it to people with whom they can form emotional bonds—skills that will be key to their success (Pink, 2005).

In essence, we are back to those three critical qualities: creativity, synthesis, and building relationships. What content or strategies will assist our students in achieving these skills? Some of the strategies, such as mind mapping, do allow students a certain amount of creativity and synthesis. They must take information, synthesize it, and create words, phrases, and pictures to represent it. Was the ability to synthesize and create already in their long-term memories and just accessed for this purpose? According to Gladwell (2008), *opportunity* is a factor in becoming successful. Students need opportunities to become creative, learn to synthesize, and create relationships with an emphasis on empathy.

Teaching Creativity

Several studies attempting to isolate areas of the brain involved in creative moments offer no specifics, but some interesting generalizations. It appears that the creative moment is related to more activity in the right hemisphere of the brain, particularly in the frontal and parietal lobes (Greenfield, 2008). Short of scanning our students' brains, how will we know when they are being creative? Wikipedia's definition as of April 2009 says creativity is "a mental and social process involving the generation of new ideas or concepts." According to Merriam-Webster's online dictionary, creativity is "marked by the ability or power to create, to bring into existence, to invest with a new form, to produce through imaginative skill, to make or bring into existence something new."

Sternberg and Grigorenko (2007) have written about successful intelligence. They say that teaching creatively means encouraging students to discover, invent, imagine, and predict. If we follow their ideas, some possible assignments for students might include the following:

- Create a different ending to the novel *The Outsiders* by S. E. Hinton. What might have happened had there not been a fire?
- Invent a different proof for the Pythagorean theory.
- Imagine what would happen if we suddenly found that there was no possible way to get access to the Internet.
- Discover the rule that governs each type of math problem.

Teaching creativity requires modeling it as well. The more creative we are in the classroom, in our lessons, and in the way we respond to our students, the more likely those mirror neurons will kick in and our students will also become more creative.

Teaming and group work also offer more opportunity for creativity. Student ideas play off each other as they work together on projects and products. Some of the Net Geners would enjoy creating products in a digital format, which could involve audio and video and come in the form of a film, an animation, a videocast, or a podcast. Eventually, publishing—in the form of a written book or video blog or a wiki—could be part of the project. Some students might create a program or even a game that would enable other students to learn material more easily and possibly make learning more fun.

Choice is a vital component of creativity. Students must have options in order for the creative process to develop. The right hemisphere sees the "big picture" and from that may come a plethora of ideas for generating some new ideas or concepts.

Teaching Synthesis

Synthesis involves summarizing, paraphrasing, and comparing and contrasting. Synthesizing requires identifying similarities and differences, which, according to Marzano, Pickering, and Pollack (2001), is the number-one way to raise student achievement. In the groundbreaking book *Classroom Instruction That Works* (Marzano, Pickering, & Pollock, 2001) and in *A Handbook for Classroom Instruction That Works* (Marzano, et al., 2001) the authors identify nine strategies that raise student achievement. These are based on a meta-analysis in which the authors looked at the results of thousands of studies. Summarizing is also on the list.

Synthesizing is like putting together pieces of a puzzle. We ask students to take new information, connect it to what they already know, and "create" something new. Every time we activate prior knowledge in our students' brains, we begin the synthesizing process.

INSTANT MESSAGE

At the beginning of every lesson, ask students to write down what they already know about the topic. Then, for each successive lesson on the topic, have them share what they already knew and what they have learned about the topic. This can be done with a think-pair-share activity, or in small groups.

As students learn information through reading, lecture, discussion, or other methods, they should take notes. Some teachers have students use a "synthesis journal." This can be set up in many ways, including the following:

• The synthesis journal may be a notebook in which the student does free writing about the topic.

• The journal may be notebook paper divided into the following three sections: What We Did, What I Learned, and How I Can Apply It.

• The journal may be an online blog. Students may take written notes in class and then write in their blogs. They may want to use sticky notes to jot down what they feel is important, organize the sticky notes, and then write in their journals.

• The journal may take the form of filling out a visual map, such as a mind map or other graphic organizer.

In Bloom's original taxonomy (Bloom & Krathwohl, 1956), synthesis was the second highest level of thinking. The ability to create was on the list of abilities under synthesis. In the new Bloom's taxonomy (Anderson & Krathwohl, 2001), the ability to create is deemed the highest level of thinking and synthesis is no longer included in the taxonomy. The change makes one think that when we teach creativity, we must also be teaching synthesis and that the reverse must also be true.

Here are some ideas for assignments that involve synthesizing:

• Based on the latest information about what is healthy for us, find a recipe that you consider "unhealthy" and replace the unhealthy ingredients with healthy ones.

• Take the information you have read in your text and in articles you have found and write an essay or article combining the authors' ideas.

• Create a movie poster for a film that combines information about the Civil War that you read in your history book and other information you found online.

• Using a story or a joke told by your teacher, paraphrase, summarize, or simply retell the story to a partner. Have the partner "fill in" any parts that he felt were missed and important enough to include.

• Using a story told or read to you by your teacher, write a moral, a theme, or a conclusion about the story.

Teaching Empathy

If you are using the teaming ideas presented in Chapter 5, you have already begun building relationships in your classroom. A vital concept in building relationships is empathy, the ability to put yourself in someone else's shoes. Empathy begins in the nursery. An infant in the hospital nursery begins to cry, and several more chime in. It's not that they are upset about being awakened or disturbed; they are actually showing signs of empathy.

What is empathy? According to Goleman (2006), empathy is the following three things:

- Knowing another person's feelings
- Feeling another person's feelings
- Responding in a compassionate manner to someone else's feelings

In our brains, an empathic response is similar to the activation of emotional contagion. When we hear a cry or see someone upset, our brains automatically not only feel empathy but also begin to imagine why the person feels the way she does. To understand how someone else feels, we use the same neural connections that were activated when we felt that way or if we were to feel that way.

Empathy is two minds with the same thoughts and feelings. Think of your favorite teacher. What made this person your favorite? Many students will tell you that the teacher understood their needs. There was a connection. You have these connections with your friends and family. But it can also happen in the classroom.

In a social studies class, the topic being discussed was terrorism. One of the students brought up the events of September 11 because an article in the paper declared that one of the suspected terrorists lived in our city. Knowing that one of my students had an uncle who died in one of the towers of the World Trade Center, I immediately glanced over at him with a heavy heart. He looked at me, and for a brief moment he knew I understood. I felt his pain. He nodded to me as if to tell me it was OK to talk about it.

When you talk to your students about empathy, assure them that we all could use practice when it comes to this particular form of emotional intelligence. There are several steps you can take in teaching them empathy:

- Share an experience in which you felt empathy for another person. Ask the students if any of them can also feel empathy for the situation that you described.
- Share a personal experience of yours in which the student might feel empathetic toward you.
- Ask students how they feel about the content you are teaching. Then, ask if others feel the same way.

By teaching and reinforcing the importance of empathy, your students will be better able to work with others in the 21st century and beyond. When people feel listened to and understood, a connection is formed that may make the difference in getting a job offer, doing well on a college interview, or just getting along with others.

How Should We Be Teaching Our Students?

The question "How should we be teaching our students?" does not have only one answer. Educational institutions have tried various ways to reach students. Some have been very successful. Some are still in the working stages. Some have fallen by the wayside.

As we consider the digital age in which we live, the demands of the 21st century, and the needs of the whole child, it is clear that we must continue to emphasize choice and balance. There are many encouraging stories about schools that make a difference. I focus here on two possible options for educating students: KIPP schools and online learning. The first keeps students within the school for longer periods of time than most other schools, and the extended time seems to make a positive difference. The second gives students the freedom to work from home or wherever an Internet connection can be found, and for some it works very well.

KIPP Schools

Bill Gates (2009) and Malcolm Gladwell (2008) cite the Knowledge Is Power Program (KIPP) as an example of good teaching and learning. The goal of this program for low-income students is to close the achievement gap and enable these students to go to college. According to Gates, a college dropout, it is imperative that children in the 21st century get a college education. According to Gladwell, these schools offer opportunity to kids who have few other resources at their disposal.

Karl Alexander and colleagues (2007) from Johns Hopkins University conducted research that showed what was causing the achievement gap between socioeconomic groups. The study determined that the biggest factor was not student ability or teaching ability; rather, it was the difference in learning over the summer. Students from wealthy families learn when they are not in school, but students from lower socioeconomic levels do not. The conclusion of this study is that schools work, but for some students there just isn't enough school.

KIPP schools overcome this deficiency. They provide students with more time in school, including longer school days and summer sessions. The school day begins at 7:25 a.m. and ends at 5:00 p.m. The students attend school every other Saturday from 9 a.m. to 1 p.m., and for three weeks during the summer they attend school from 8 a.m. to 2 p.m. Ninety-four percent of students who attend a KIPP middle school get a scholarship to a private or parochial high school and then have an 80 percent chance of going to college, compared with the national average of 40 percent.

Students begin their day with a 30-minute class on thinking skills. Every day they have 90 minutes of math, 90 minutes of English, an hour of social studies, and an hour of science. Everyone gets music instruction at least twice a week, and all students take orchestra. There are extracurricular activities after school and sports teams as well.

Teachers are well trained. With the extra time each day for math and English, teachers can actually slow the pace and allow students the time they need to learn and retain information.

Online Learning

When I typed in the words "online learning" to do a Google search, I got a few million "hits." Online learning is not just one thing. Online learning includes Web sites for kids, toddlers, preschoolers, elementary school students, and high school students. Educational sites, educational games, and any type of learning that can be done on the World Wide Web is considered online learning.

More than 30 percent of students in the United States never finish high school. The dropout rate is climbing, and online learning may be one solution to the problem. Students drop out of school because they are bored, are unsuccessful, or need to work to earn money. The possibility of taking courses for credit online is appealing to many of our students. Home-schoolers often opt for online courses.

Online learning offers several advantages: learning at your own pace, stopping and reviewing when necessary; learning "on the road," wherever there is an Internet connection; and having one-on-one online conferences with your instructor. Some programs offer more interactive opportunities than the traditional classroom. Many public and private high schools offer some of their courses online. One option for students is to take some of their required or optional graduation credits online from their own high school. Teachers learn a new way of teaching when they design and run these classes.

There are also virtual high schools that offer accredited diplomas online. In this case, the student might complete an entire high school course load online and receive a diploma this way. Virtual high school courses have been around for many years and have offered students in small rural schools the opportunity to take courses that their schools would never be able to offer (Tinker, 1998).

Some virtual schools offer a kindergarten through 8th grade curriculum. For example, the Chicago Virtual Charter School offers both a K–8 program and a high school program. Only about 20 percent of the classes in the elementary program are delivered online. The rest are to be administered by adults with materials provided by the program. The charter school Web site and links to samples can be accessed through this web address: www.k12.com/cvcs.

Is online learning the wave of the future? Perhaps. Teachers can now receive advanced degrees completely online. Some educators question the validity of such degrees. I spoke to some college professors about online degrees, and most admitted that the time has come to accept online learning degrees as being equal to traditional degrees.

Years ago, my hesitation about online and distance learning rested on what I knew about brain research. Is online learning brain compatible? The answer appears to be "it depends." Courses that include regular interaction among participants and online conferences between teacher and student seem to follow the principle of "brains learn better with other brains." If an Internet-based phone system such as Skype is used so that the conferencing includes some face-to-face time via video-conferencing, that is even better. Add the use of Web sites, blogs, and the social messaging application Twitter, and the class participants will be linked more often and more closely in "real" time.

As technology becomes more affordable and accessible, more learning will take place in this way and perhaps in more sophisticated formats.

NOT JUST ANOTHER TEXT MESSAGE

 Relationships among students are important to learning. The digital brain belongs in your classroom and in our new world. Try to recognize the gifts technology brings to extend your students' learning. Offer students choices that include digital media, but always be aware that the whole child needs balance. The citizens of the world whose brains we are helping design need guidance in making some of their choices. By providing both high-tech options and face-to-face encounters to enhance their learning, we can give them a world of information that will help them become creative and respectful, with the ability to synthesize information and share it with others. The knowledge they seek can be combined with the emotional wisdom they will need to make the decisions that will shape their lives. They are 21st century brains; they are the future.

APPENDIX A

How the Brain Works

At birth the brain weighs only about one pound, but it contains an astronomical number of brain cells called neurons. You are born with approximately 100 billion neurons. Fortunately, they are so small that about 30,000 of these will fit on the head of a pin. In the last few years, scientists have realized that the brain continuously goes through a process of cell regeneration called neurogenesis. In other words, the brain was once thought to be unable to produce new neurons, but that has been proven false. This new discovery suggests the promising possibility of replacing neurons that have been damaged or destroyed.

Neurons are the cells that do the communicating in the brain. Each neuron can communicate with many others; in fact, every neuron may have 100,000 connections (Ratey, 2001). The neurons send messages to one another in a specific way to allow you to do all the things that you must get done. They take in information and cause the responses to that information.

The structure of neurons has been compared to trees, lollipops, broccoli, and various other objects. I prefer to explain their structure and function by having you simply look at your hand, palm up. Your palm represents the cell body with its nutrients, DNA, and chemicals. Your fingers are the dendrites of this brain cell. Dendrites take information into the cell through tiny openings called receptors. Information is sent to the dendrites in the form of chemicals, but as the chemicals attach themselves to the dendrites, the message becomes electrical. This electrical message goes through the cell body and along your forearm, which represents the structure called the axon. Many axons are coated with a white fatty substance called myelin. Among its many functions, myelin helps messages travel safely and quickly. At the end of the axon are vesicles that contain chemicals called neurotransmitters. The electrical impulse causes the vesicles to open, forcing the neurotransmitter out through the end of the axon. So it's in through the dendrite and out through the axon. The neurotransmitters are either reabsorbed by the sending neuron when they have completed their job or an enzyme breaks them down.

Although neurons can grow many dendrites, they have only one axon. If the axon is used often, it will grow little terminals to allow more flow of information. When the message reaches the end of the axon, in order to attach itself to the next neuron, it must cross a chemical gap called a synapse. Figure A.1 illustrates neurons communicating in this way.

When neurons communicate, they are said to "fire." Although there is always electrical activity in the brain—that is, neurons are usually emitting low levels of electrical activity—when neurons are not firing rhythmically and purposefully, they are said to be "at rest." Neurons that fire together in a pattern are called neural networks. These networks form the patterns and programs in our brains. Thus, a thought requires a network of neurons to fire. There are millions of these networks in your brain.

Neurons are not the only cells in the brain. In fact, they make up only 10 percent of the three-pound mass of an adult brain. The other 90 percent consists of glial cells. These glia are support cells. One type of glia, oligodendrocytes, actually forms the myelin sheath around the axon. They wrap themselves around this nerve fiber to assist with transmission of messages at a rate 100 times faster than the rate of axons that are not coated.

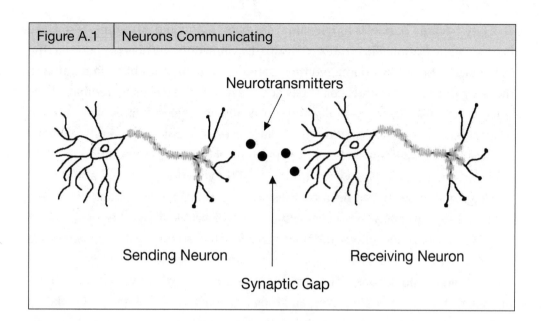

| Figure A.1 | Neurons Communicating |

Neurotransmitters

Sending Neuron

Synaptic Gap

Receiving Neuron

They also play a key role in learning and memory. For instance, your memory of a birthday party includes visual, auditory, and kinesthetic components. As you formed this memory, the components were separated in your brain; the visual parts were stored in the visual cortex, the sounds were stored in the auditory cortex, and so on. As you recall this memory, all of the component parts are brought together in the frontal lobe of your brain. They must all converge at the same time in order for the memory to make sense to you. It appears that the myelin (those glial cells) synchronizes the transmission so that the information that comes from the farthest points can arrive along with the other sensory information (Fields, 2008).

The Importance of Making Connections

Neuroscientist David Snowdon (2001) studied an order of nuns living in Mankato, Minnesota, whose longevity appeared to surpass that of most other people. These women were living independently with little difficulty into their 90s and 100s. Snowdon wanted to know why they were doing so well, and what their brains looked like. So these nuns, and others who were a part of their order, donated their brains to science.

They became part of a longitudinal study on aging and Alzheimer's disease funded by the National Institutes of Health. Dr. Snowdon and his colleagues at the University of Kentucky conducted this examination of mental ability in relation to the aging process. The study continues and the results have been incredible. These women remained active mentally and physically until their deaths. What is even more revealing is that according to the autopsies some of them had Alzheimer's disease, but they did not show many symptoms of this terrible condition.

The women's lifestyles were studied, and they were questioned about their upbringing. It appears that because these women remained active and continued to learn, they had many more connections in their brains than other people their ages. With a lot of connections, the brain can afford to lose some without manifesting symptoms of dementia. The women's lifestyle adds to their longevity. They all have the same goals and purpose. They live in the "slow lane," their lives are less stressful than many other people's lives, and they have each other's support. In relation to the many connections in their brains, they have an enriched environment. They play games, read, work on puzzles, work in the community, and contribute to the functioning of the order.

There also appeared to be a direct relationship between the women's level of education and the complexity of their brains. Those with higher levels of education and more complex jobs showed more brain growth with more connections. The nuns with less formal education and more mundane jobs had fewer connections.

Neurotransmitters

There are about 50 or 60 known neurotransmitters, but let's take a look at just a few. Because we will be looking at memory and mood later on, it will be necessary to understand what a few of these chemicals do in the brain and the body.

When it comes to memory, we must first look at the neurotransmitter acetylcholine. This is one of the most abundant chemicals in your brain. Without it, it is not possible to form long-term memories. This is the chemical that is in short supply in Alzheimer's patients. Factual memories are processed in the structure called the hippocampus, and this is where most acetylcholine is found. This chemical appears to increase when we sleep, and most scientists believe that this is the time that information is practiced and stored by the brain. Acetylcholine is also released through movement. This suggests a very good reason to add movement to learning.

Serotonin is a calming neurotransmitter. Production of serotonin takes place in brain regions located just above the spinal cord, but the serotonin-producing neurons have very long axons. Serotonin, consequently, may be involved in almost every message sent. It is one of several neurotransmitters called neuromodulators, because they assist in carrying messages in many areas of the brain. Serotonin regulates mood. It has been implicated in many areas of our lives. It is associated with migraine headaches, premenstrual syndrome, menopause, and depression. There are many different types of serotonin, which probably explains its involvement in so many things. High levels of serotonin are found in people with high self-esteem. Low levels are found in those who have trouble handling relationships, are impulsive, and are sometimes violent. There are many antidepressants prescribed to modulate the amount of serotonin in the brain. These are called specific serotonin reuptake inhibitors (SSRIs). You are probably familiar with the names Prozac, Paxil, and Zoloft. These are popular SSRIs. They allow better availability of serotonin in the synapses by preventing this chemical from being reabsorbed into the sending neuron. Serotonin is also involved in our appetite and our sleep.

Melatonin is a neurotransmitter that has been acclaimed as providing a fountain of youth. In reality, it is related to sleep. Melatonin is released in the middle of the brain, and it causes drowsiness. Our biological clock activates its release. Many believe that the amount of light we are exposed to at the time we usually go to sleep may be a factor when we have trouble sleeping. Our sleep-deprived students may be spending too much time in front of a computer or television screen, which delays the release of melatonin and their ability to fall asleep. Melatonin is sometimes prescribed to treat sleep disorders, and many travelers take this over-the-counter product to deal with jet lag.

Endorphins are chemicals that are involved in our feeling of well-being. These are the body's own natural painkillers, and they got their name from the fact that they are endogenous morphine. When we are in physical or emotional pain, endorphins are released and make us feel better. It is said that during childbirth a woman's endorphin levels kick into overdrive at a level of about 100 times their normal rate. This chemical also helps us focus and concentrate.

Norepinephrine is an excitatory neurotransmitter. That means its effect is causing neurons to fire. This chemical is released whenever something unusual happens. It gets our attention and affects our heart rate and breathing. Also a neuromodulator, norepinephrine is found in many areas of the brain. Too much norepinephrine can cause hypervigilance; too little is implicated in depression.

Most of us have heard of the chemical dopamine. This is the neurotransmitter involved in Parkinson's disease. It is a calming, or inhibitory, chemical that stops neurons from firing. In the case of Parkinson's, not enough dopamine is released in an area of the brain called the basal ganglia. Because the neurons in this area are not kept from firing, people with the disease have tremors and jerky movements. If you are sitting quietly while reading this book, your dopamine is working nicely and allowing you to do so.

Dopamine is also involved in other areas of the brain with different results. It is part of the reward system in the brain. Almost every addictive substance affects the release of dopamine. In an area of the brain called the ventral tegmental area, dopamine gives a feeling of pleasure. Think of your favorite food. (Mine would be warm chocolate chip cookies.) Did you get a nice feeling from the thought? Dopamine was released in your brain by thinking about something that gives you pleasure. Eating, sex, shopping, or gambling may cause a dopamine rush. The implications of this are astounding. Drug addicts who are off of their drug of choice can get that rush from walking by the place where they used to buy their drugs. The feeling makes them want their drug again. This is why it is so difficult to get "unhooked."

Dopamine is also a major player in the part of our brains that helps us focus and make decisions. Just as an air traffic controller lets some planes land and holds others back, dopamine controls brain activity so we can pay attention to one thing at a time. This also allows us to make a decision and stick to it. Did you ever have to make up your mind and have a tough time doing so? A shortage of dopamine at that time could have been the problem. Students with attention deficit disorder (ADD) or attention deficit hyperactivity disorder (ADHD) have lower levels of dopamine in their frontal lobes. Ritalin and other drugs for the disorder increase the amount of this neurotransmitter in the synapses of this brain area.

GABA and glutamate are two other neurotransmitters worth mentioning. GABA (gamma-aminobutyric acid) is a calming neurotransmitter. It helps keep the brain from becoming overstimulated. It is implicated in chronic anxiety. Valium, a well-known tranquilizer, works on GABA. Glutamate is an excitatory neurotransmitter that is present in many areas of communication in the brain. Glutamate and GABA, with other chemicals, try to keep the brain in a homeostatic or balanced state.

Your brain is an electrochemical soup pot of sorts. When all of the right amounts of chemical and electrical activity are present, the brain runs in a very systematic pattern. If these chemicals get out of balance—and they are influenced by everything we eat, say, and do—then we might run into some problems.

Brain Structures

At conception, the brain is nothing more than a neural tube. As it grows, the neurons migrate to certain areas of the brain to become part of a specific structure. The lower part of the brain is called the brain stem. It consists of several structures that help regulate the body. The medulla oblongata, the pons, and the reticular activating system are all located here. The reticular activating system, or RAS, is the first filter for incoming information. All sensory information, except for the sense of smell, enters the brain through the brain stem. The RAS keeps you alert to new, unusual, or important information, but it filters out many of the redundant messages that would overwhelm you.

From the brain stem, information is sent to an area of the brain generally called the limbic system. This system involves several structures, one of which is called the thalamus. This is the second filter for information. The thalamus sorts the information to send it to appropriate places in the brain. For instance, visual input would be sent to the back of the brain, to the visual cortex. It is thought that the thalamus may have an important function in regulating the electrical activity in the brain as well. When the thalamus sorts information, it sends factual information that is going to be stored in long-term memory to the hippocampus. This structure is shaped like a seahorse and catalogs all of our facts. It doesn't hold every factual memory, but acts more like a card catalog at the library and categorizes them. If information is of an emotional nature, it is sent to a small almond-shaped structure called the amygdala, which catalogs emotional content.

The hypothalamus is another structure in the limbic system. Just as the thalamus sorts information coming from outside the body, the hypothalamus sorts internal information. It is in charge of hunger, thirst, and sex drive. This little formation also initiates the stress response by sending a message to the pituitary gland, which is located close by. This gland receives the message and releases chemicals that affect the adrenal glands, which are located above the kidneys.

Memories are stored in different areas of the brain. The top layer of brain, the part that we always see as wrinkled and folded, is called the cerebral cortex. This is divided into two hemispheres and four lobes. At the back of the brain are the occipital lobes. They are responsible for processing visual information. At the top of the brain toward the back are the parietal lobes. These areas process touch and spatial information. On either side of the head above the ears are the temporal lobes. They process speech and hearing. The frontal lobes, located at the front of the brain, are in charge of future planning, decision making, abstracting, and problem solving. It is in this area that dopamine helps us make up our minds and stick to it. In people with attention deficit disorder, it is this area of the brain that is lacking sufficient dopamine to help them focus. There may also be other chemicals, such as serotonin, that are out of balance. Figure A.2 provides a graphic of how this process works.

A Brief Look at Phineas Gage

The part of the frontal lobes located behind the forehead is called the prefrontal cortex. This is a highly specialized area that deserves some attention. It is here that the brain has its scratchpad, which is what working memory is sometimes called. This memory system holds on to new information for short periods of time for our conscious mind to consider. This scratchpad becomes larger and more capable throughout the brain's development. The prefrontal cortex also deals with our emotions and, as a result, affects our personality.

| Figure A.2 | How Memories Are Reconstructed |

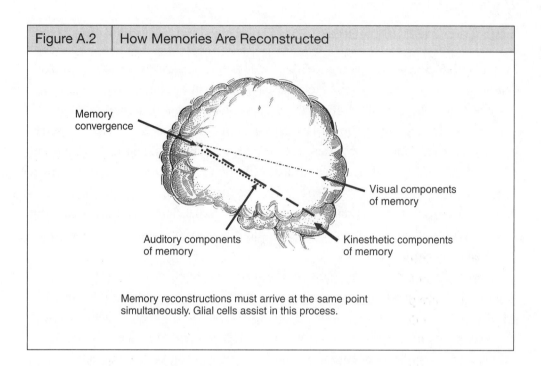

Memory convergence

Visual components of memory

Auditory components of memory

Kinesthetic components of memory

Memory reconstructions must arrive at the same point simultaneously. Glial cells assist in this process.

In 1848 there was a railroad worker named Phineas Gage. His job was to tamp down gunpowder with a three-foot iron rod so workers could blow away rock and debris in order to lay down track. While Phineas was doing his job one day, the gunpowder exploded. As a result, the iron rod shot out of his hands and went through his cheek and out of the top of his head! Amazingly, Phineas survived. After weeks of bed rest, Phineas went back to work; however, his personality had completely changed. From an easygoing, lovable man emerged a mean person who used foul language. His behavior was so bad that he lost his job and his wife.

When his brain was examined after his death, scientists realized that the prefrontal cortex was damaged. This is the part of the brain that controls the emotional center, the amygdala. Without the control from this intellectual part of the brain, emotions tend to run the brain and can cause problems. The tragedy of Phineas Gage gave us important information about the function of the brain.

The Two Hemispheres

Perhaps you have been called a "left-brained" person or a "right-brained" person. These designations refer to the fact that each hemisphere has specific functions. The left hemisphere controls the right side of the body, and the right hemisphere controls the left side of the body. The left hemisphere is associated with language, details, math, and analyzing, whereas the right hemisphere deals with music, art, whole ideas, and spatial representations. Although each hemisphere has its own functions, the brain is very "plastic." This means that areas will compensate in function for areas that are unable to perform their tasks. This plasticity allows the brain to grow and change as we learn new things. It also gives us the power to make changes in our own brains.

The two hemispheres are connected by a structure called the corpus callosum. It allows the two hemispheres to communicate. The idea of being right-brained or left-brained is sort of a hare-brained idea! Both hemispheres are involved in almost everything we do. For instance, although the left hemisphere is usually in charge of language, it supplies only the words and the sequence; it is the right hemisphere that provides the affect, or expression, in our voices.

We can't leave this discussion of the brain without mentioning the structure located at the bottom of the back of the brain called the cerebellum. Previously it was thought to control only posture and balance. In recent years, researchers have discovered that the cerebellum does much more. It is involved in learning and memory, as well as storage of long-term and permanent memories. It is filled with very active neurons that process information at an enormous rate.

How Tech Savvy Are You?

----- 🌐 -----

You've now read quite a bit about the new brain. You've thought about how old you are and which generation you fit into. How do you feel about this? Where do you stand and where do you want to be? In the checklist below, place a check next to the statements that are true about you. Copy the checklist and distribute it to your students to find out how tech-savvy they are. Consider whether you want to catch up to them. And let them teach you for a change.

__ 1. I have a personal e-mail account.

__ 2. I have a cell phone that I have turned on most of the time.

__ 3. I have sent text messages on my phone.

__ 4. I have received text messages on my phone.

__ 5. I have a personal blog.

__ 6. I read others' blogs.

__ 7. I use my e-mail account often.

__ 8. I send and receive instant messages on my computer.

__ 9. I have and use an interactive whiteboard in my classroom.

__ 10. I use the Internet for research.

__ 11. I shop on the Internet.

__ 12. I play computer games.

__ 13. I spend more than two hours per day on the computer.

__ 14. I play games on other digital media such as PlayStation, Nintendo, or Wii.

__ 15. I like to check my e-mail at least once daily.

__ 16. I have used technology in my teaching.

__ 17. I have had a videophone conversation using Skype and a webcam.

__ 18. I have a Twitter account.

__ 19. I own an MP3 player.

__ 20. I download podcasts.

Glossary of Digital Terms

blog—"Web log"; journal entries that are posted on a Web site and updated on a regular basis (visit blogger.com)

cyberspace—electronic medium of computers

e-mail—way of sending text messages via the Internet

Facebook—social networking Web site that began as a private community and has gone public

icon—visual representation, usually of a file on a computer; any visual that represents a message or a feeling, such as a smiley face

interactive whiteboard—large white screen connected to a computer and capable of projecting anything that appears on the computer screen, allowing projected images to be manipulated with fingers, special pens, or other devices

MySpace—highly customizable social networking Web site that allows interaction with a network of friends

podcast—personal on demand (pod) broadcasting of digital files (programs) that can be downloaded to listen to or watch anytime

Skype—software application that enables phone calls to be made over the Internet and with the use of a webcam, so callers are visible

Twitter—online service that allows people to share short updates of what is going on in their life (visit twitter.com)

webcam—small camera that usually attaches to a computer monitor and allows video to be sent over the Internet; can be used for video chat sessions

wiki—Web site whose users can add and edit content; a page for organizing and coordinating information; wiki is a Hawaiian word for "fast"

YouTube—Web site where users can upload and view short video clips

References

Alexander, K. A., Entwisle, D. R., & Olsen, L. S. (2007, April). Lasting consequences of the summer learning gap. *American Sociological Review, 72,* 167–180.

Allen, L., Nickelsen, L., & Zgonc, Y. (2007). *Prepping the brain: Easy and effective ways to get students ready for learning.* San Clemente, CA: Kagan Publishing.

Anderson, L. W., & Krathwohl, D. R. (Eds.). (2001). *A taxonomy for learning, teaching and assessing: A revision of Bloom's taxonomy of educational objectives.* New York: Longman.

Associated Press. (2006, October 6). Stanford University study warns of internet addiction. Retrieved August 15, 2009, from http://abclocal.go.com/kabc/story?section=news/local&id=4679518.

Begley, S. (2007). *Train your mind, change your brain: How a new science reveals our extraordinary potential to transform ourselves.* New York: Ballantine Books.

Black, P., & Wiliam, D. (1998, October). Inside the black box: Raising standards through classroom assessment. *Phi Delta Kappan, 80*(2), 139–144.

Bloom, B. S., & Krathwohl, D. R. (1956). *Taxonomy of educational objectives: The classification of educational goals, by a committee of college and university examiners. Handbook 1: Cognitive domain.* New York: Longman.

Bonnet, M. H., & Arand, D. L. (1995, December). We are chronically sleep deprived. *Sleep, 18*(10), 908–911.

Buzan, T. (2006). *Mind mapping: Kickstart your creativity and transform your life.* London: BBC Active.

Caine, G., & Caine, R. (1994). *Making connections, teaching and the human brain.* New York: Innovative Learning Publications.

Castleman, B., & Littky, D. (2007, May). Learning to love learning. *Educational Leadership, 64*(8), 58–61.

Commission on the Whole Child. (2007). *The learning compact redefined: A call to action.* Alexandria, VA: ASCD.

Committee on Public Education. (2001, February). American Academy of Pediatrics: Children, adolescents, and television. *Pediatrics, 107*(2), 423–426.

Davis, A., & McGrail, E. (2009, March). The joy of blogging. *Educational Leadership, 66*(6), 74–77.

Derbyshire, D. (2009). Social websites harm children's brains: Chilling warning to parents from top neuroscientist. Retrieved August 14, 2009, from http://www.dailymail.co.uk/news/article-1153583/Social-websites-harm-childrens-brains-Chilling-warning-parents-neuroscientist. html.

Doidge, N. (2007). *The brain that changes itself.* New York: Penguin.

Elias, M. J., & Arnold, H. (Eds.). (2006). *The educator's guide to emotional intelligence and academic achievement: Social-emotional learning in the classroom.* Thousand Oaks, CA: Corwin Press.

Elias, M. J., Zins, J. E., Weissberg, R. P., Frey, K. S., Greenberg, M. T., Haynes, N. M., et al. (1997). *Promoting social and emotional learning: Guidelines for educators.* Alexandria, VA: ASCD.

Eliot, L. (1999). *What's going on in there? How the brain and mind develop in the first five years of life.* New York: Bantam Books.

Estes, D. (2008). Brain-compatible teaching [Presentation]. ASCD's 2008 Annual Conference. New Orleans, LA.

Fields, R., (2008, March). White matter matters. *Scientific American, 298*(3), 54–61.

Gardner, H. (1983). *Frames of mind.* New York: Basic Books

Gardner, H. (2006). *Multiple Intelligences: New Horizons.* New York: Basic Books

Gardner, H. (2007). *Five minds for the future.* Cambridge, MA: Harvard Business School Press.

Garner, B. (2008). *Getting to got it.* Alexandria, VA: ASCD.

Gates, W. (2009). Bill Gates on mosquitos, malaria and education. Retrieved March 30, 2009, from www.ted.com/talks/lang/eng/bill_gates_unplugged.html

Gazzaniga. (1999). *The mind's past.* Berkley, CA: University of California Press.

Gelb, M.J., (1998). *How to think like Leonardo da Vinci.* New York: Delacorte Press.

Gladwell, M. (2008). *Outliers: The story of success.* New York: Little, Brown.

Glenn, H. S. (1990). *The greatest human need.* [Video recording]. Gold River, CA: Capabilities, Inc.

Goldin-Meadow, S., Cook, S., & Mitchell, Z. (2009, March). Gesturing gives children new ideas about math. *Psychological Science, 20*(3), 267–72.

Goleman, D. (1996). *Emotional intelligence.* New York: Bantam.

Goleman, D. (2006). *Social intelligence.* New York: Bantam.

Greenfield, S. (2008). *The quest for identity in the 21st century.* London: Hodder & Stroughton.

Hattie, J., & Timperley, H. (2007). The power of feedback. *Review of Educational Research, 77*(1), 81–112.

Healy, J. (1998). *Failure to connect.* New York: Simon and Schuster.

Healy, J. (2004). *Your child's growing mind.* New York: Broadway Books.

Iacoboni, M. (2008). *Mirroring people: The new science of how we connect with others*. New York: Macmillan

Jensen, E. (2005). *Teaching with the brain in mind* (2nd ed.). Alexandria, VA: ASCD.

Kagan, J., & Herschkowitz, N. (2005). *A young mind in a growing brain*. New York: Lawrence Erlbaum.

Klingberg, T. (2008). *The overflowing brain*. New York: Oxford University Press.

Lantieri, L. (2008). *Building emotional intelligence*. Louisville, CO: Sounds True.

Littky, D., & Castleman, B. (2007, May). Learning to love learning. *Educational Leadership, 64*(8), 58–61

Malyarenko, T., Kuraev, G., Malyarenko, Y., Khatova, M., Romanova, N. G., & Gurina, V. I. (1996). The development of brain electric activity in 4-year-old children by long term stimulation with music. *Human Physiology, 22*, 76–81.

Margulies, N. (2002). *Mapping inner space: Learning and teaching visual mapping*. Tucson, AZ: Zephyr Press.

Markova, D., & Powell, A. (1998) *Learning unlimited*. Berkeley, CA: Conari Press.

Marzano, R. J., Norford, J. S., Paynter, D. E., Pickering, D. J., & Gaddy, B. D. (2001). *A handbook for classroom instruction that works*. Alexandria, VA: ASCD.

Marzano, R. J., Pickering, D. J., & Pollack, J. E. (2001). *Classroom instruction that works*. Alexandria, VA: ASCD.

Medical News Today. (2008, March 5). Arts and cognition research released by Dana Foundation. Article adapted by *Medical News Today* from original press release. Available from: http://www.medicalnewstoday.com/articles/99577.php.

Medina, J. (2008). *Brain rules*. Seattle, WA: Pear Press.

Nunley, K. (2007). *Differentiating for the high school student*. Thousand Oaks, CA: Corwin Press.

Oxford University Press. (2006, September 20). First evidence that musical training affects brain development in young children. *ScienceDaily*. Retrieved April 22, 2009, from http://www.sciencedaily.com /releases/2006/09/060920093024.htm.

Patoine, B. (2008, March 4). Research consortium finds new evidence linking arts and learning. BrainWork. Dana Foundation. Available from http://www.dana.org/news/brainwork/detail.aspx?id=11604.

Payne, R. (1998). *A framework for understanding poverty*. Highlands, TX: RFT Publishing.

Pink, D. (2005). *A whole new mind: Moving from the information age to the conceptual age*. New York: Riverhead Books.

Ratey, J. (2001). *A user's guide to the brain*. New York: Pantheon Books.

Ratey, J. J. (2008). *Spark: The revolutionary new science of exercise and the brain*. New York: Little, Brown.

Rogers, S. (2008). Reinventing classroom assessment to increase achievement with challenging students [Presentation]. ASCD's 2008 Annual Conference. New Orleans, LA.

Rose, C., & Nicholl, M. (1997). *Accelerated learning for the 21st century*. New York: Dell Publishing.

SAGE Publications/Psychology of Music. (2009, March 16). Music education can help children improve reading skills. *ScienceDaily*. Retrieved April 22, 2009, from http://www.sciencedaily.com/releases/2009/03/090316075843.htm.

Scott, S. (2006). The myth of multitasking. *Chatelaine*. Available from: http://www.scottreports.com/journalism/Sarah_Scott-The_Myth_of_Multi-Tasking.pdf.

Small, G., & Vorgan, G. (2008). *iBrain: Surviving the technological alteration of the modern mind.* New York: Harper Collins.

Snowdon, D. (2001). *A matter of grace.* New York: Bantam Books.

Sprenger, M. (1999). *Learning and memory: The brain in action.* Alexandria, VA: ASCD.

Sprenger, M. (2005). *How to teach so students remember.* Alexandria, VA: ASCD.

Sprenger, M. (2006). *Becoming a "wiz" at brain-based teaching: How to make every year your best year.* Thousand Oaks, CA: Corwin Press.

Sprenger, M. (2008). *The developing brain.* Thousand Oaks, CA: Corwin Press.

Sternberg, R. J. (1996). *Successful intelligence.* New York: Simon & Schuster.

Sternberg, R., & Grigorenko, E. (2007). *Teaching for successful intelligence to increase student learning* (2nd ed.). Thousand Oaks, CA: Corwin Press.

Stiggins, R. (2001). *Student-involved classroom assessment* (3rd ed.). Upper Saddle River, NJ: Merrill Prentice Hall.

Stipek, D. (2006, September). Relationships matter. *Educational Leadership, 64*(1), 46–49.

Stone, L. (2007). Linda Stone's thoughts on attention. Available from: http://www.lindastone.net/

Sylwester, R. (2006, February). Mirror neuron update. Available from: http://www.brainconnection.com/content/226_1.

Tapscott, D. (2009). *Grown up digital: How the net generation is changing your world.* New York: McGraw-Hill.

Tinker, R. (1998). *The virtual high school™: A scalable cooperative.* Concord, MA: Concord Consortium.

Tomlinson, C. (1999). *The differentiated classroom.* Alexandria, VA: ASCD.

University of Minnesota Digital Center. (n.d.). Mind-mapping tool. Available from: http://dmc.umn.edu/objects/mindmap/.

University of Rochester. (2007, July 28). Hand gestures dramatically improve learning. *ScienceDaily*. Available from: http://www.sciencedaily.com/releases/2007/07/070725105957.htm.

van Duijvenvoorde, A. C. K., Zanolie, K., Rombouts, S. A. R. B., Raijmakers, M. E. J., & Crone, E. A. (2008, September 17). Evaluating the negative or valuing the positive? Neural mechanisms supporting feedback-based learning across development. *The Journal of Neuroscience, 28*(38), 9495–9503.

Webb, D., & Webb, T. (1990). *Accelerated learning with music.* Norcross, GA: Accelerated Learning Systems.

Wiley-Blackwell. (2009, February 11). Adolescents involved with music do better in school. *ScienceDaily*. Retrieved April 22, 2009, from http://www.sciencedaily.com/releases/2009/02/090210110043.htm.

Wiliam, D. (2008, March 17). Classroom assessment: minute by minute, day by day [Presentation]. ASCD's 2008 Annual Conference. New Orleans, LA.

Willis, J. (2006). *Research-based strategies to ignite student learning: Insights from a neurologist and classroom teacher.* Alexandria, VA: ASCD.

Wolf, M. (2007). *Proust and the squid.* New York: Harper.

Wolfe, P. (2001). *Brain matters.* Alexandria, VA: ASCD.

Wong, P., Skoe, E., Russo, N., Dees, T., & Kraus, N. (2007). Musical experience shapes human brainstem encoding of linguistic pitch patterns. *Nature Neuroscience, 10,* 420–422.

Zull, J. (2002). *The art of changing the brain: Enriching the practice of teaching by exploring the biology of learning.* New York: Stylus Publishing.

Index

Note: Page numbers followed by *f* indicate a figure.

171

About the Author

M arilee Sprenger is an educational consultant specializing in brain research applications, differentiation, and learning and memory. She is a member of the American Academy of Neurology, an adjunct professor at Aurora University, and an international professional development specialist.

She has taught in primary, middle, and secondary settings. She has written numerous articles online and in journals, and she is the author of six other books: *Learning and Memory, The Brain in Action, Becoming a "Wiz" at Brain-Based Teaching, Differentiation Through Learning Styles and Memory, How to Teach So Students Remember, Memory 101 for Educators,* and *The Developing Brain.*

Through her work she would like to ensure that all educators teach to the whole child with the brain in mind.

You can reach her by mail at 5820 North Briarwood Lane, Peoria, IL, 61614; by phone at (309) 692-5820; and by e-mail at brainlady@gmail.com.

Related ASCD Resources: Brain-Based Teaching

At the time of publication, the following ASCD resources were available; for the most up-to-date information about ASCD resources, go to www.ascd.org. ASCD stock numbers are noted in parentheses.

Print Products

Brain-Friendly Strategies for the Inclusion Classroom by Judy Willis (#107040)

Brain Matters: Translating Research into Classroom Practice by Patricia Wolfe (#101004)

Educational Leadership, September 2009, Teaching for the 21st Century (#110020)

Education Update, June 2005, Mental Mileage (#105113)

How to Teach So Students Remember by Marilee Sprenger (#105016)

Research-Based Strategies to Ignite Student Learning: Insights from a Neurologist and Classroom Teacher by Judy Willis (#107006)

The Strategic Teacher: Selecting the Right Research-Based Strategy for Every Lesson by Harvey F. Silver, Richard W. Strong, and Matthew J. Perini (#107059)

Teaching Every Student in the Digital Age: Universal Design for Learning by David H. Rose, Anne Meyer, Nicole Strangman, and Gabrielle Rappolt (#101042)

Video

Teaching the Adolescent Brain Video Series (one DVD with three 30-minute programs and one 15-minute program with a comprehensive facilitator's guide) (#406050)

PD Online Courses

The Brain: Understanding the Mind (#PD04OC44)

The Brain: Understanding the Physical Brain (#PD99OC05)

The Brain: Memory and Learning Strategies (#PD02OC18)

THE WHOLE CHILD The Whole Child Initiative helps schools and communities create learning environments that allow students to be healthy, safe, engaged, supported, and challenged. To learn more about other books and resources that relate to the whole child, visit www.wholechildeducation.org.

For additional resources, visit us on the World Wide Web (http://www.ascd.org), send an e-mail message to member@ascd.org, call the ASCD Service Center (1-800-933-ASCD or 703-578-9600, then press 2), send a fax to 703-575-5400, or write to Information Services, ASCD, 1703 N. Beauregard St., Alexandria, VA 22311-1714 USA.